Feed my Best Friend Better: Simple, Nourishing Recipes and Treats for Dogs

Daniel J. Sanford

Published by Gordon Nsowine, 2023.

FEED MY BEST FRIEND BETTER: SIMPLE, NOURISHING RECIPES AND TREATS FOR DOGS

First edition. November 19, 2023.

ISBN: 979-8223874829

Written by Daniel J. Sanford.

Simple, Nourishing Recipes
And Treats For Dogs

FEED MY BEST FRIEND BETTER

Simple, Nourishing Recipes
And Treats For Dogs

DANIEL J. SANFORD

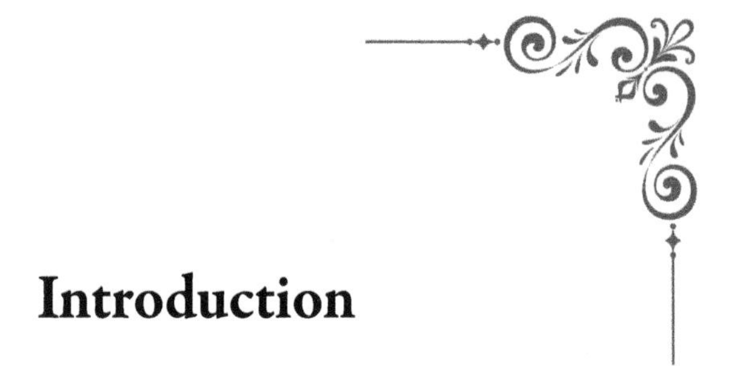

Introduction

IT'S LIKELY THAT IF you're reading this book, you adore your dog and want to give them the greatest nourishment and care available. It is not just you. A study conducted by the American Pet Products Association found that 68% of dog owners purchase treats for their pets, and 85% of dog owners view their pets as members of the family. But are you really aware of what's actually in the dog food and treats you give him? Are you familiar with their selection, preparation, and storage methods? Do you know how to alter them to suit the requirements and tastes of your dog? Do you know how to accomplish this while saving time and money?

Don't panic if you said "no" to any of these inquiries. You can get aid from this book. This book will teach you how to make homemade dog food and treats for your greatest buddy, so that you can feed them better. You will learn about the advantages of feeding your dog homemade food and treats, as well as the fundamentals of dog nutrition, how to prepare and store dog food, how to make dog food recipes for all occasions and seasons, how to make dog treats and snacks, how to shop for dog food on a budget, and how to answer frequently asked questions about homemade dog food.

Why should you prepare your own dog treats and food at home? Though there are many, the following are some of the most significant ones:

Your dog's health and enjoyment can be enhanced with homemade dog food and treats. Artificial colors, flavors, preservatives, fillers, by-products, and allergens are just a few of the dangerous ingredients that can be found in commercial dog food and treats. These ingredients can lead to a number of health concerns for your dog, including diabetes, obesity, allergies, digestive disorders, skin, dental, and even cancer. However, fresh, natural, healthful, and balanced ingredients and supplements included in homemade dog food and treats will strengthen your dog's immune system, metabolism, energy, mood, and general well-being.

Your dog's requirements and preferences can be catered to with homemade dog food and treats. It's possible that commercial dog treats and food don't suit your dog's unique dietary needs and preferences. For instance, a dog's age, size, breed, exercise level, and health issues can all affect how many calories, protein, fat, or carbohydrates they require. Certain dogs may also have dietary intolerances or allergies that necessitate avoiding particular substances. Additionally, certain dogs could be finicky eaters, favoring particular food flavors, textures, or forms. Conversely, you may tailor your dog's diet to suit their unique requirements and tastes by using homemade dog food and treats. You have the ability to select the best ingredients and supplements for your dog, modify the food's flavors, textures, and forms, and change the macronutrient and micronutrient quantities and ratios.

You may cut costs and save time by making your own dog food and treats. Commercial dog food and treats can be pricey, particularly if you purchase premium, organic, or high-quality brands. However, if you buy in bulk, use coupons, and check costs, homemade dog food and treats may end up being less expensive. Additionally, you can make use of seasonal ingredients or leftovers that you already have in your kitchen or can simply and affordably purchase. You can save time by making your own dog food and treats, particularly if you prepare ahead of time, cook in bulk, and freeze your dog's food. You can also employ straightforward recipes with few materials, equipment, and stages. Additionally, you can prepare your dog's meals and treats ahead of time and store them carefully for later use.

How can homemade dog treats and food be prepared? It's not as difficult as you may believe. Everything you need to know and do to prepare your own homemade dog food and treats is contained in this book.

You will learn how to make homemade dog food and treats for your closest buddy and will feel more confident after reading this book. Making your own homemade dog food and treats will also be enjoyable, both in the process and the finished product. Experimenting with various ingredients, recipes, and techniques will be enjoyable. Positive changes in your dog's behavior, happiness, and health will also be evident to you. Additionally, you'll fortify your relationship and mutual trust with your dog.

So, why do you hesitate? Gather your ingredients, your dog, your apron, and your utensils, and let's get cooking!

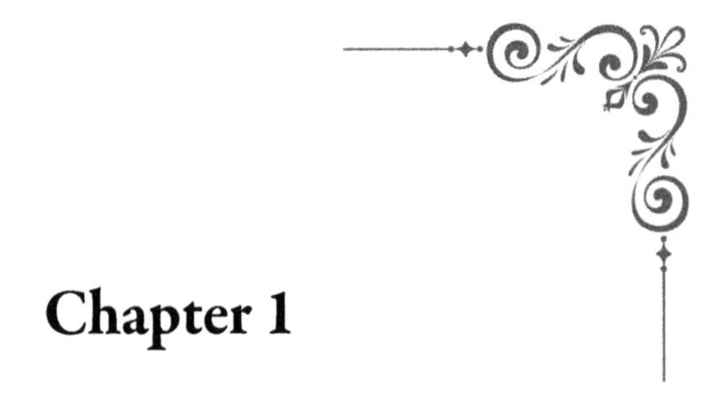

Chapter 1

The Benefits of Homemade Dog Food

YOU WILL READ MORE about the benefits of homemade dog food and treats over store-bought options in this chapter. Along with learning typical dangers and mistakes to avoid while creating homemade dog food, you will also learn how to select the proper ingredients and supplements for your dog's diet.

How Homemade Dog Food Can Improve Your Dog's Health and Happiness

Your dog's health and happiness can be enhanced by making your own homemade dog food and treats, which is one of the key reasons to do so. Commercial dog food and treats could include dangerous additives that put your dog at risk for obesity, diabetes, allergies, digestive disorders, skin disorders, dental disorders, and even cancer. However, fresh, natural, healthful, and balanced ingredients and supplements included in homemade dog food and treats will strengthen your dog's immune system, metabolism, energy, mood, and general well-being.

The following are some advantages of homemade dog treats and food for your dog's wellbeing:

Make-your-own dog food and treats can help avoid or lessen obesity. Dog obesity is a prevalent and dangerous health issue, particularly in developed nations. In 2018, 56% of dogs in the US were overweight or obese, per a research by the Association for Pet Obesity Prevention. Dogs that are obese may experience a number of health issues, including diabetes, rheumatoid arthritis, heart disease, respiratory issues, and shortened lifespans. Your dog can maintain a healthy weight by eating homemade dog food and treats, which provide the proper quantity and quality of calories, protein, fat, and carbohydrates. Additionally, you have the ability to regulate the amount and timing of your dog's meals and snacks so that you don't overfeed or underfeed them.

Make-your-own dog food and treats can help minimize or avoid allergies. Another prevalent and dangerous health issue that affects dogs, particularly in industrialized nations, is allergies. A research conducted by the American Animal Hospital Association found that 20% of dogs in the US had environmental allergies and 10% of dogs have food allergies. Dogs with allergies may exhibit a range of symptoms, including licking, biting, skin infections, ear infections, hair loss, and gastrointestinal issues. Because homemade dog food and treats contain hypoallergenic ingredients and vitamins, they can help your dog avoid or minimize allergies. Additionally, you can reduce or completely remove allergens including wheat, maize, soy, dairy, eggs, cattle, chicken, pig, seafood, and artificial additives from your dog's diet.

Handcrafted dog food and treats help minimize or avoid stomach problems. Another prevalent and significant health concern in dogs, particularly in developed nations, is digestive disorders. A research conducted by the American Veterinary Medical Association found that 15% of dogs in the country have long-term digestive problems, including colitis, gastritis, pancreatitis, and gastroenteritis. Dogs with digestive problems may exhibit a range of symptoms, including diarrhea, vomiting, constipation, gas, bloating, and abdominal pain. Because homemade dog food and treats contain easily digested nutrients and minerals, they can help prevent or lessen digestive problems in dogs. Additionally, you can maximize the amount of fiber, hydration, and probiotics in your dog's diet and minimize or stay away from foods that might aggravate or upset their stomach, such fatty, spicy, or spoilt food.

Dog treats and food created at home might lessen or avoid skin issues. Another prevalent and severe health issue in dogs, particularly in industrialized nations, is skin issues. A research conducted by the

American Kennel Club found that dermatitis, pyoderma, mange, hot spots, and fungal diseases affect 25% of dogs in the US. Dogs with skin issues may exhibit a range of symptoms, including redness, swelling, dryness, flakiness, scabs, sores, and odors. Giving your dog homemade dog food and treats with wholesome ingredients and supplements might help prevent or lessen skin issues in your dog. In addition, you may improve your dog's skin and coat health by supplementing his diet with vital fatty acids, vitamins, minerals, and antioxidants. You should also restrict or stay away from items like sugar, salt, and artificial additives that can aggravate or exacerbate skin issues.

Tooth issues in dogs can be avoided or minimized with homemade dog food and treats. For dogs, dental issues are another prevalent and dangerous health issue, particularly in wealthy nations. A research conducted by the American Veterinary Dental Society found that by the time a dog reaches the age of three, 80 percent of them in the US had periodontal disease. Dogs suffering with periodontal disease may have a range of symptoms, including painful gums and teeth, plaque, tartar, gingivitis, tooth decay, and loss of teeth. By giving your dog crunchy and chewy ingredients and supplements, homemade dog food and treats can help prevent or lessen dental problems. Additionally, you can help your dog's oral hygiene by adding natural antibacterial and anti-inflammatory ingredients to their food, like parsley, mint, coconut oil, and turmeric, as well as limiting or avoiding foods high in sugar, starch, and artificial additives, which can aggravate or cause dental issues.

Dog treats and food created at home help lessen or prevent cancer. For dogs, cancer is the most common cause of death, particularly in affluent nations. A research conducted by the Morris Animal Foundation found that 50% of dogs in the US over 10 will have cancer. A collection of illnesses known as cancer are caused by the aberrant division and development of cells, which can harm or even kill the body's healthy tissues and organs. Because homemade dog food and treats contain anti-cancer chemicals and supplements, they can help your dog prevent or lessen cancer. Along with limiting or avoiding foods that can cause or encourage cancer, such as processed meat, smoked or charred food, artificial additives, and spinach, kale, broccoli, cranberries, mushrooms, garlic, ginger, and green tea, you can also help prevent cancer in your dog by adding natural anticancer and immune-boosting ingredients to their diet.

As you can see, feeding and treating your dog at home can benefit their health and happiness in a number of ways. You can make sure your dog receives the greatest nutrition and care possible by producing their own homemade dog food and treats. In addition, there are numerous common and major health issues that can be prevented or treated to enhance the quality and length of a dog's life.

How to Choose the Right Ingredients and Supplements for Your Dog's Needs.

Making your own homemade dog food and treats allows you to select the proper ingredients and supplements for your dog's needs, which is another reason to do so. It's possible that commercial dog treats and food don't suit your dog's unique dietary needs and preferences. For instance, a dog's age, size, breed, exercise level, and health issues can all affect how many calories, protein, fat, or carbohydrates they require. Certain dogs may also have dietary intolerances or allergies that necessitate avoiding particular substances. Additionally, certain dogs could be finicky eaters, favoring particular food flavors, textures, or forms. Conversely, you may tailor your dog's diet to suit their unique requirements and tastes by using homemade dog food and treats. You have the ability to select the best ingredients and supplements for your dog, modify the food's flavors, textures, and forms, and change the macronutrient and micronutrient quantities and ratios.

When selecting the components and add-ons for your dog's meal, keep the following things in mind:

The amount of calories and nutrients that your dog needs. Your dog's calorie and nutritional needs should be your first priority when selecting the ingredients and supplements for their meal. The energy that your dog needs in order to go about their everyday business is measured in calories. The things your dog needs in order to stay healthy and happy are called nutrients. Your dog requires water, protein, fat, carbs, vitamins, and minerals as its primary nutrients. Your dog's nutritional requirements and energy intake are determined by a number of factors, including breed, age, size, activity level, and overall health. Dogs with specific health conditions may require more or less of a given nutrient than healthy dogs, and puppies require more calories and protein than adult dogs, large dogs require more calories and nutrients than small dogs, and active dogs require more calories and carbohydrates than sedentary dogs. If you want to know how many calories and nutrients your dog needs, you can utilize online calculators or speak with your veterinarian. To find out how many calories and nutrients are in the ingredients and supplements you use to make your dog's meal, you can also utilize nutrition labels or internet databases. To ensure that your dog's food is meeting their calorie and nutrient requirements, you can then modify the quantity and caliber of the foods and supplements you use.

Your dog's dietary intolerances or allergies. Your dog's dietary allergies or intolerances should be the second thing you take into account when selecting the components and additives for their meal. Food allergies refer to anomalous immune responses to certain food proteins, which can result in a range of symptoms for your dog, including but not limited to itchiness, licking, biting, skin infections, ear infections, and gastrointestinal issues. Food intolerances are abnormal reactions of the digestive system to specific food ingredients. Your dog may have a variety of symptoms, including diarrhea, vomiting, constipation, gas, bloating, and pain in the abdomen. For dogs, wheat, corn, soy, dairy, eggs, beef, chicken, pork, fish, and artificial additives are the most prevalent food allergies and intolerances. However, depending on your dog's specific sensitivity, any food may result in an allergic or intolerance reaction. To find out which foods your dog is allergic to or has intolerances to, you can utilize allergy testing or elimination diets. Additionally, you may keep an eye on your dog's symptoms and how different diets affect him. Next, you can reduce or remove any possible allergies or intolerances from your dog's diet and swap them out with hypoallergenic or easily digested foods.

Your dog's taste preferences. Your dog's taste preferences should be the third thing you take into account when selecting the components and additives for their diet. Your dog's taste preferences refer to the flavors, textures, and forms of food that they prefer or reject. Numerous factors, including heredity, experience, environment, and temperament, might influence one's taste preferences. For instance, whilst some dogs enjoy flavors that are sweet, sour, or bitter, others may favor flavors that are meaty, savory, or salty. While some dogs could like textures that are harsh, dry, or crunchy, others might prefer textures that are soft, wet, or silky. While some dogs enjoy food that is irregular, flat, or stick-shaped, others may prefer food that is round, square, or bone-shaped. Additionally dynamic, taste preferences can shift over time based on how your dog is exposed to and adjusts to various meals. To find out what tastes your dog prefers, you might experiment or observe them. For advice or information about your dog's taste preferences, you can also get in touch with the breeder, shelter, or prior owner of your dog. Then, you can adjust the flavors, textures, and forms of the products and supplements you use for your dog's food, as well as limit or avoid any ingredients that your dog rejects or detests, to suit their tastes.

You may prepare your own homemade dog food and treats that are tailored to your dog's needs and tastes by taking these aspects into account while selecting the proper ingredients and supplements for their diet. Making your own homemade dog food and treats is a fun way to bond with your dog and a great way to guarantee that they receive the best possible nutrition and care.

How to Avoid Common Pitfalls and Mistakes When Making Homemade Dog Food

MAKING YOUR OWN DOG food and treats allows you to avoid frequent problems and mistakes. This is another reason to create your own dog food. The safety and quality of commercial dog treats and food may be compromised, endangering the health and wellbeing of your canine companion. For instance, certain commercial dog treats and food may include bacteria, fungi, parasites, poisons, or other objects that might injure, poison, or cause diseases in your dog. In addition, certain commercial dog treats and food may be recalled or taken off the market because of flaws, mistakes, or infractions that put your dog's health and welfare in jeopardy. On the other hand, you can prevent or reduce the risks and hazards that may emerge from using commercial dog food and treats by making your own, giving you more control over the food's safety and quality.

When preparing homemade dog food and treats, keep in mind the following typical hazards and errors:

use dangerous or subpar vitamins and chemicals. Using inferior or dangerous products and supplements is one of the major traps and blunders that you should avoid when making homemade dog food and treats. Ingredients and supplements that are past their expiration date, ruined, rotten, moldy, rancid, stale, or otherwise inappropriate for eating are considered low-quality or unsafe. Your dog may have a number of issues from infection, poisoning, indigestion, vomiting, diarrhea, and allergic reactions to low-quality or dangerous components and supplements. For your dog's food, you should only use fresh, natural, wholesome, and balanced ingredients and supplements that are appropriate for your dog's diet. Avoid using cheap or dangerous ingredients and supplements. The components and supplements you use for your dog's food should also have their expiration dates, labels, and seals checked. You should also store these items correctly and hygienically to keep them from degrading or spoiling.

use dangerous or unsuitable supplements and chemicals. When creating homemade dog food and treats, using the wrong or dangerous ingredients and supplements is another typical mistake to avoid. Supplements and components that are toxic, poisonous, or detrimental to dogs in any other way are considered inappropriate or dangerous. Your dog may have a range of issues from vomiting and diarrhea to constipation, gas, bloating, abdominal pain, liver damage, kidney damage, nerve damage, and even death if they consume inappropriate or dangerous foods and supplements. It is advisable to solely utilize safe, healthful, and advantageous foods and supplements that are acceptable for your dog's meal rather than any improper or hazardous ones. Additionally, you should minimize or stay away from foods and supplements that are unsuitable for dogs in their diet. Chocolate, grapes, raisins, onions, garlic, chives, macadamia nuts, xylitol, alcohol, caffeine, avocado, mushrooms, salt, sugar, artificial additives, and human pharmaceuticals are a few of the substances and supplements that are unsuitable or dangerous for dogs.

use partial or out-of-balance vitamins and substances. Using inadequate or unbalanced ingredients and supplements is another typical mistake to avoid when creating homemade dog food and treats. Supplements and components that don't give your dog the right number and quality of calories and nutrients are considered unbalanced or incomplete. Inadequate or unbalanced components and supplements can lead to a number of issues for your dog, including toxicity, excess, insufficiency, and malnourishment. Only balanced and complete ingredients and supplements that are appropriate for your dog's food should be used; steer clear of unbalanced or incomplete ingredients and supplements. In order to meet your dog's calorie and nutritional needs, you should also pay attention to the guidelines and recommendations on the amount and quality of products and supplements you use in your dog's diet. If you need any help or guidance on how to properly balance and supplement your dog's diet, you should also speak with your veterinarian or a canine nutritionist.

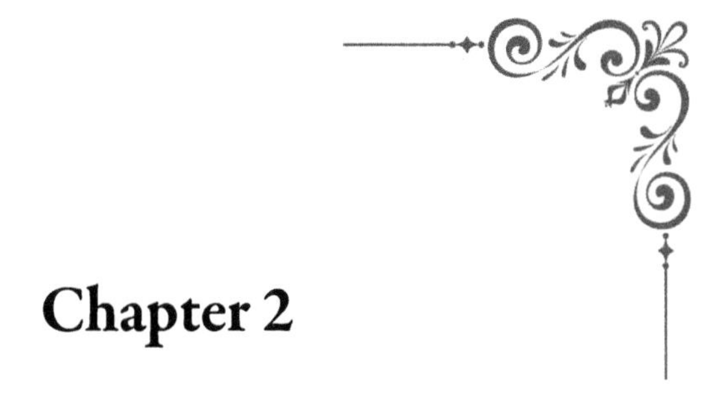

Chapter 2

The Basics of Dog Nutrition

How to Understand and Calculate Your Dog's Calorie and Nutrient Requirements

A further step in creating your own homemade dog treats and food is to make sure your dog's diet is balanced with both macro and micronutrients. The macronutrients—protein, fat, and carbs—are the kinds of nutrition that your dog requires in high concentrations. Micronutrients, which include vitamins, minerals, and water, are the nutrients that your dog requires in trace amounts. The health and wellbeing of your dog depend on both macronutrients and micronutrients, each of which plays a distinct role in your dog's body. As a result, you should feed your dog the right ratio and proportion of each nutrient and balance the quantity and quality of macronutrients and micronutrients in their diet.

The following are some suggestions and guidelines for ensuring that the macro- and micronutrients in your dog's food are balanced:

Maintain a balanced protein intake for your dog. The vitamin known as protein gives your dog's body its building blocks, including muscles, hormones, enzymes, amino acids, and antibodies. Additionally, protein is the food that gives your dog's body energy, particularly in situations where there is not enough fat or carbohydrate available. The most vital nutrient for dogs is protein, which should account for 18% to 25% of their diet, depending on their size, age, breed, degree of activity, and overall health. High-quality, complete protein sources, such meat, chicken, fish, eggs, and dairy products, are what you should feed your dog since they give all the important amino acids that dogs require. To guarantee that your dog receives a varied and well-balanced diet of amino acids, you should also offer them a range of protein sources. Additionally, you ought to stay away from or restrict your dog's intake of incomplete and low-quality protein sources, such as grains, legumes, nuts, and seeds, since they may include anti-nutritional elements that might impede your dog's ability to digest and absorb protein. Additionally, these sources may lack some of the important amino acids your dog requires.

Don't overindulge in fat for your dog. Depending on your dog's age, size, breed, activity level, and overall health, fat should account for 10% to 15% of their diet. Fat is the nutrient that gives your dog's body the most concentrated source of energy. Additionally, fat is the nutrient that gives your dog's body the vital fatty acids, including omega-3 and omega-6, that are involved in a number of different processes and functions, like immunity, inflammation, healthy skin and coats, and the development of the brain and nerves. Additionally, fat is the nutrient that gives your dog's body the fat-soluble vitamins, such A, D, E, and K, which are critical for blood coagulation, bone health, antioxidant protection, and eyesight. High-quality, well-balanced fat sources, like plant, fish, and animal oils, are ideal for giving your dog. These sources provide the proper ratio and quantity of important fatty acids and fat-soluble vitamins. To guarantee that your dog receives a varied and well-balanced diet of vitamins and fatty acids, you should also give them access to a range of fat sources. Additionally, you ought to stay away from or restrict your dog's intake of low-quality, unbalanced fat sources like vegetable oils, margarine, and shortening. These sources can be harmful to your dog's health because they contain trans fats or oxidized fats, as well as excessive or insufficient amounts of the fat-soluble vitamins or essential fatty acids that your dog needs.

Make sure your dog's diet is balanced with carbohydrates. Depending on your dog's age, size, breed, activity level, and overall health, carbohydrates should make up between 30% and 50% of their diet. Carbohydrates are the food that gives your dog's body its energy most quickly. The component that gives your dog's body its fiber, which is necessary for proper digestion, bowel movements, and blood sugar balance, is carbohydrates. Additionally, your dog's body needs carbohydrates to produce water-soluble vitamins like B and C, which are critical for immune system function, metabolism, and antioxidant defense. Treat your dog to a diet rich in complex carbohydrates, such as fruits, vegetables, and whole grains, along with the appropriate kind and quantity of fiber and water-soluble vitamins. In order to guarantee that your dog receives a varied and well-balanced diet of vitamins and fiber, you should also offer them a range of carbohydrates. Additionally, you should limit or stay away from low-quality, simple carbohydrate sources like sugar, honey, molasses, and refined grains. These sources can cause your dog to become obese, diabetic, or develop dental issues. They can also contain excessive amounts of fiber or water-soluble vitamins, empty calories, or a high glycemic index.

Make sure your dog's diet is vitamin-balanced. Vitamins are the nutrients that your dog's body uses as coenzymes or cofactors. They are important for a number of bodily processes and functions, including development, immunity, growth, metabolism, and antioxidant protection. Water-soluble and fat-soluble vitamins are the two categories into which vitamins are divided. Vitamins A, D, E, and K are among the fat-soluble vitamins that are kept in your dog's body fat. Vitamins B and C are examples of water-soluble vitamins, which are those that are not stored in the body of your dog. Water-soluble and fat-soluble vitamins each have distinct roles and activities in your dog's body, but they are both necessary for good health. It's important to provide your dog the right quantity of fat-soluble and water-soluble vitamins in a balanced ratio, and to prevent or treat any excess or deficiency of any vitamin. Along with natural and bioavailable vitamin sources like fruits, vegetables, meat, eggs, and dairy products, you should also limit or avoid synthetic or artificial vitamin sources like supplements, additives, and fortifiers that may contain contaminants, impurities, or additives that could be harmful to your dog's health. Before giving your dog any vitamin supplements, you should also speak with your veterinarian or a canine nutritionist. This is because certain vitamins can be poisonous or harmful to dogs if given in excess or in the wrong way.

Maintain a balanced mineral intake for your dog. Minerals are the nutrients that provide your dog's body with structural or functional elements. They are involved in many different processes and functions, including the development of bones and teeth, the contraction of muscles, the transmission of nerve signals, the activation of enzymes, and the maintenance of fluid equilibrium. There are two categories for minerals: **macrominerals and microminerals.** The minerals known as macrominerals, which include calcium, phosphorus, magnesium, sodium, potassium, and chloride, are necessary for your dog in significant proportions. The minerals that your dog requires in trace levels are called microminerals, and they include iron, zinc, copper, manganese, selenium, iodine, and cobalt. Although they play different roles in your dog's body, macrominerals and microminerals are both vital to their health and wellbeing. Both macrominerals and microminerals should be given to your dog in sufficient and balanced proportions, and any excess or shortage in any one mineral should be avoided. Additionally, you should limit or avoid giving your dog access to synthetic or artificial sources of minerals, such as supplements, additives, or fortifiers, which may contain contaminants, impurities, or additives that could be harmful to their health. Instead, you should give them natural and bioavailable sources of minerals, such as meat, bones, eggs, dairy products, and sea vegetables. Before giving your dog any mineral supplements, you should also speak with your veterinarian or a canine nutritionist. This is because certain minerals can be toxic or hazardous to dogs if given in excess or in the wrong way.

Maintain a balance of water in your dog's diet. The nutrient that makes up between 60% and 70% of your dog's body is water, which is essential for controlling body temperature, blood circulation, waste removal, and nutrient absorption, among other processes. The most vital nutrient for your dog is water, which should account for 70% to 80% of their diet, depending on their size, age, breed, degree of activity, and overall health. It is recommended to give your dog access to clean, fresh, and filtered water; do not use tap, bottled, or distilled water since these sources may include impurities, chemicals, or minerals that could be harmful to your dog's health. In addition, you should always provide your dog water, keep an eye on their intake and output, and prevent or treat dehydration or overhydration. If your dog exhibits any indications of a water imbalance, such as dry lips, sunken eyes, lethargy, panting, vomiting, diarrhea, or seizures, you should also speak with your veterinarian or a canine nutritionist.

You may provide your dog the best nutrition and care possible by adhering to these recommendations and standards for balancing macronutrients and micronutrients in their food. In addition, there are numerous common and major health issues that can be prevented or treated to enhance the quality and length of a dog's life.

How to Adjust Your Dog's Diet According to Their Age, Size, Breed, Activity Level, and Health Conditions

A further step in creating your own homemade dog food and treats is to modify your dog's diet based on their breed, age, size, amount of exercise, and health. These elements may impact your dog's nutritional and energy needs, as well as their taste preferences and any dietary intolerances or allergies. As a result, you should adjust your dog's diet to fit their unique requirements and features and give them the best nutrition and care possible.

The following are some pointers and recommendations for changing your dog's food based on their size, age, breed, degree of exercise, and health:

Your dog's food should be modified based on their age. The growth, development, immunity, metabolism, and age of your dog can all have an impact on how many calories and nutrients they need. For instance, in order to sustain their rapid growth and development, pups require higher levels of protein and calories than adult dogs. In order to avoid obesity and constipation, senior dogs require less calories and more fiber than adult dogs. Depending on your dog's life stage, you need modify their food to give them the right quantity and kind of calories and nutrients. If you would want any help or advice on feeding your dog appropriately for their age, you should also speak with your veterinarian or a canine nutritionist.

Adapt your dog's diet to their weight. The energy expenditure, appetite, and body composition of your dog can all be impacted by their size, which in turn can change how many calories and nutrients they need. For instance, in order to maintain their larger body mass and higher energy expenditure, giant dogs require more calories and nutrients than tiny dogs. To maintain their higher metabolism and lean body mass, little dogs require more protein and fewer calories than large dogs. Your dog's diet should be modified to give them the right quantity and quality of calories and nutrients based on their body weight and body condition score. For more guidance or help on feeding your dog based on their size, speak with your veterinarian or a canine nutritionist.

Your dog's diet should be modified based on their breed. The genetic predisposition, physical attributes, behavioral features, and consequently the amount of calories and nutrients required for your dog can all be influenced by their breed. For instance, some breeds might be more or less energetic, grow more quickly or more slowly, have longer or shorter hair coats, or have more or fewer health issues than others. Your dog's diet should be modified based on breed-specific requirements and traits, and you should give them the right kind and quantity of calories and nutrients. For additional help or guidance on feeding your dog according to their breed, speak with your veterinarian or a canine nutritionist.

Adapt your dog's diet to their amount of exercise. Your dog's activity level can have an impact on their need for calories and nutrients as well as their energy consumption, muscle mass, and endurance. For instance, in order to fuel their increased energy consumption and preserve their muscular mass and endurance, active dogs require higher calorie and carbohydrate intakes than sedentary dogs. To avoid obesity and maintain their muscle mass and power, dogs that are not active require more protein and less calories than those that do. Your dog's diet should be modified to suit their activity regimen and lifestyle, and you should give them the right kind and quantity of calories and nutrients. For further guidance or help on feeding your dog based on their activity level, speak with your veterinarian or a canine nutritionist.

Adapt your dog's food to their specific medical needs. The illnesses affecting your dog may have an impact on their immunity, metabolism, digestion, and absorption of nutrients, which may change how much calories and nutrients they need. For instance, your dog may need to consume more or less of a particular nutrient than usual if they have diabetes, kidney disease, liver disease, or cancer. A special or therapeutic diet may also be necessary for your dog to manage certain medical issues, such as pancreatitis, inflammatory bowel disease, food allergies, or obesity. Your dog's diet should be modified in accordance with their medical diagnosis and treatment plan, and you should provide them the right kind and quantity of calories and nutrients. For additional guidance or support on feeding your dog in accordance with their medical needs, speak with your veterinarian or a canine nutritionist.

You can provide your dog the best nutrition and care possible by modifying their food to suit their age, size, breed, activity level, and health issues by using these pointers and recommendations. In addition, there are numerous common and major health issues that can be prevented or treated to enhance the quality and length of a dog's life.

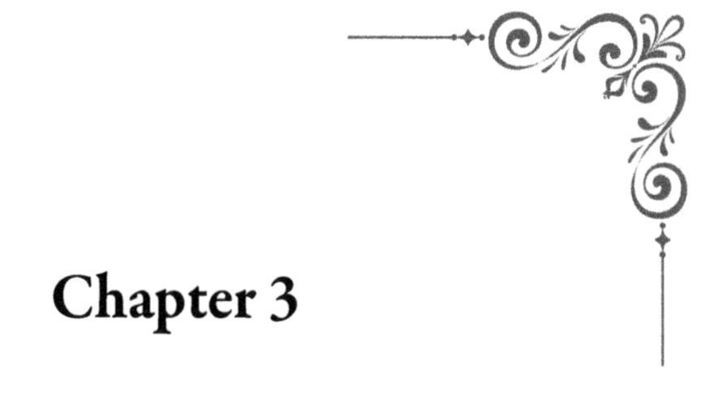

Chapter 3

The Essentials of Dog Food Preparation and Storage

THIS CHAPTER WILL COVER the practical aspects of preparing and storing dog food, including how to safely and hygienically cook, portion, and serve your dog's meals; how to conveniently store, freeze, and thaw your dog's meals; and how to use and clean your kitchen tools and equipment.

How to Cook, Portion, and Serve Your Dog's Meals Safely and Hygienically

COOKING, PORTIONING, and serving your dog's food in a safe and hygienic manner is one of the tasks involved in creating your own homemade dog food and treats. In addition to ensuring that your dog receives the most nutrition and enjoyment from their food, safe and hygienic cooking, portioning, and serving techniques can help minimize or lower your dog's risk of contracting infections, illnesses, or injuries from contaminated food. In addition to ensuring that your dog's food stays fresh, delicious, and enticing, safe and hygienic cooking, portioning, and serving practices can help minimize or lessen the danger of cross-contamination, spoiling, or waste.

The following advice can help you prepare, portion, and serve your dog's food in a safe and hygienic manner:

Cook the food for your dog until it's evenly cooked. By cooking your dog's food thoroughly and evenly, you may make it safer, simpler for him to digest, and eliminate any harmful bacteria, parasites, or poisons that might be present in the raw components. In addition to improving the food's flavor, texture, and appearance, properly and evenly cooking it will also make it more enticing and fulfilling for your dog. By utilizing the proper cooking technique, temperature, time, and equipment for each ingredient and adhering to the directions and guidelines for each dish, you can ensure that your dog's food is cooked thoroughly and uniformly. Additionally, you should use a thermometer, a knife, a fork, or your senses to check the doneness and quality of your dog's food. It's important to prevent overcooking or undercooking your dog's food because this can have an impact on its nutritional value and palatability.

Make sure you correctly and appropriately portion your dog's food. By correctly and appropriately portioning your dog's food, you can prevent or lessen obesity, malnutrition, excess, imbalance, and deficiency in your dog, as well as give them the proper quantity and quality of calories and nutrients. In addition to preventing or reducing overfeeding or underfeeding, precisely portioning your dog's food will guarantee that your dog receives the best possible nutrition and care. By using the proper measurement equipment, such as cups, spoons, scales, or containers, and by adhering to the suggested and computed amounts of calories and nutrients for your dog, you may portion your dog's food correctly and precisely. In addition, you should modify the amount of food your dog eats based on their size, age, breed, activity level, and health. If you need any help or advice with meal preparation, speak with your veterinarian or a canine nutritionist.

Give your dog his food on time and correctly. In addition to giving your dog the finest nutrition and enjoyment from their food, correctly and promptly serving it will also help avoid or lessen any problems or complications that may occur from giving your dog their meal in an improper or untimely manner. In addition to preventing or minimizing spills, waste, and mess, giving your dog their food in a timely and appropriate manner helps maintain its freshness, flavor, and attractiveness. Serving your dog's food correctly and promptly means using the right serving utensils, including bowls, plates, trays, or mats, and paying attention to the directions and specifications for every recipe. Along with serving food at the proper temperature, consistency, and frequency, you should also steer clear of or restrict your dog's consumption of any hot, cold, dry, or wet food items that could irritate or damage their mouths, stomachs, or intestines. In addition, you should feed your dog at the proper time, location, and manner and minimize or eliminate any disruptions, games, or other activities that can interfere with their hunger, digestion, or behavior.

How to Store, Freeze, and Thaw Your Dog's Meals Properly and Conveniently

STORING, FREEZING, and thawing your dog's meals in an easy-to-access manner is a crucial step in creating your own homemade dog food and treats. It is possible to maintain the safety and quality of your dog's food as well as minimize or prevent spoilage, contamination, and degradation by correctly and efficiently freezing and thawing your dog's meals. You can save time and money by properly and conveniently freezing and thawing your dog's meals, as well as guaranteeing that your dog always has access to fresh, delicious, and visually appealing food.

The following are some pointers and ideas for conveniently storing, freezing, and thawing your dog's meals:

Food for your dog should be kept in leak-proof, sealed bags or containers. Food for dogs should be stored in leak-proof, airtight containers or bags to prevent or minimize exposure to air, moisture, or bacteria and to extend its freshness and safety. Food for your dog should be kept in leak-proof, airtight bags or containers made of food-grade materials like metal, plastic, or glass that you can reuse and clean easily. Along with labeling the food's name, date, and ingredients, you should also pay attention to the shelf lives and expiration dates of the products and supplements you use to make your dog's food.

If you plan to keep your dog's food longer than three days, freeze it. By freezing your dog's food, you can increase its shelf life by up to six months and stop or lessen any bacterial, fungal, or parasitic development or activity that could be present in it. If you want to create big batches of your dog's food ahead of time or want to store it for longer than three days, you should freeze it. To facilitate the process of defrosting and serving your dog's food, it is advisable to freeze it in small, discrete servings. In order to maintain the freshness and quality of your dog's food, you should freeze it as soon as it is cooked.

Give your dog's food a slow, safe thaw. Safely and gently thawing your dog's food can help to preserve its flavor and texture as well as minimize any loss or damage to the nutrients or water in it. One of the following techniques should be used to safely and gradually thaw your dog's food:

The safest and most advised way to defrost your dog's food is to use a refrigerator. This method maintains the food at a steady, low temperature while inhibiting the growth or activity of any bacteria, fungi, or parasites that could be present. Depending on its size and thickness, your dog's food should be refrigerated for a minimum of 12 to 24 hours to defrost. In order to minimize or stop food leakage, you should also put your dog's food in a shallow, covered container or bag. It is recommended that you utilize your dog's food within three days of it thawing in order to minimize the risk of spoiling or contamination.

The cold water method is a quicker and more practical way to thaw your dog's food, but it needs more care and attention because it exposes the food to higher and more fluctuating temperatures, which raises the possibility of bacteria, fungi, or parasites growing or becoming active in the food. Depending on how big and thick your dog's food is, you should thaw it in cold water for anywhere from thirty to sixty minutes. Additionally, you ought to store your dog's food in a waterproof, sealed container or bag to minimize or avoid any food-water contact. In order to maintain clean, cold water, you need also change the water every thirty minutes. It is advisable to utilize your dog's food as soon as it thaws in order to minimize or avoid spoiling or contamination.

The microwave method is the quickest and most straightforward way to thaw dog food, but it is also the least advised since it exposes the food to high and uneven temperatures, which results in the greatest loss or damage to the food's nutrients or water content. Depending on the size and thickness of the food, you should microwave it for five to ten minutes to thaw it for your dog. To lessen the chance of your dog's food exploding or spattering, you should also put it in a vented, microwave-safe container or bag. Additionally, to guarantee that your dog's food is thoroughly and evenly thawed, you should rotate or mix it every few minutes. Additionally, as soon as the food has thawed, you should utilize it for your dog to avoid or minimize spoiling or contamination.

These pointers and advice will help you to correctly and conveniently store, freeze, and defrost your dog's meals while giving them the healthiest possible diet and maximum enjoyment from their food. In addition, there are numerous common and major health issues that can be prevented or treated to enhance the quality and length of a dog's life.

How to Use and Clean Your Kitchen Tools and Equipment Effectively and Efficiently

USING AND CLEANING your kitchen gear and equipment effectively and efficiently is another stage in creating your own homemade dog food and treats. In addition to preventing or minimizing food waste, contamination, and damage, you may enhance the quality and safety of your dog's food by using and cleaning your kitchen gear and equipment with effectiveness and efficiency. You may save time and money by using and cleaning your kitchen tools and equipment effectively and efficiently, which will help keep your kitchen functional, tidy, and clean.

The following are some pointers and recommendations for efficiently and successfully utilizing and cleaning your kitchen items and equipment:

For any task, use the appropriate tools and equipment. Your cooking procedure can be made simpler, quicker, and more accurate by using the appropriate tools and equipment for each activity. This will also guarantee that your dog's food is cooked, portioned, and served in a hygienic and proper manner. Knives, cutting boards, spoons, cups, scales, bowls, plates, trays, mats, pots, and pans, ovens, microwaves, refrigerators, freezers, and containers are among the tools and equipment you should need for each operation. You should also pay attention to the directions and guidelines provided for each dish. Additionally, you want to utilize easily cleaned and easily operated tools and equipment composed of materials safe for usage around food, like silicone, glass, ceramic, or stainless steel. Additionally, you want to stay away from or utilize less tools and equipment that are difficult to use or clean, made of shoddy or dangerous materials like plastic, wood, or metal.

After every usage, make sure your tools and equipment are clean. Cleaning your tools and equipment both before and after each use will help to keep them clean and fresh for longer by preventing or reducing the buildup of dirt, grease, or bacteria. Before and after each use, you should clean your tools and equipment by following the manufacturer's instructions and guidelines and using the proper cleaning technique, such as washing, rinsing, drying, or sanitizing. To properly and gently clean your instruments and equipment, you should also use soap, detergent, or bleach, as well as clean, hot water and a sponge, towel, or brush. In addition, you should minimize or stay away from using harsh or abrasive chemicals, unclean or cold water, or rough or sharp things to clean your tools and equipment because they can cause scratches or other damage.

Keep your equipment and tools organized and in good condition. Tools and equipment can be kept dry and safe for extended periods of time by being stored neatly and appropriately, which can also limit or minimize any exposure to air, moisture, or pests. It is important to keep your tools and equipment organized and in good condition by using the right storage techniques (such as hanging, stacking, or nesting) and adhering to the care instructions and specifications for each piece of equipment. When storing tools and equipment that is not in use, you should use airtight, leakproof containers or bags and mark them with the name and date of the item. Additionally, keep your tools and equipment out of direct sunlight, extreme heat, and moisture by storing them somewhere dry and cold. Additionally, you should try to keep your tools and equipment away from heat sources, moisture, electricity, and water.

You may provide your dog the finest nutrition and food delight possible by using and cleaning your kitchen items and equipment correctly and efficiently by adhering to these recommendations and ideas. In addition, there are numerous common and major health issues that can be prevented or treated to enhance the quality and length of a dog's life.

Chapter 4

The Recipes of Dog Food for Every Occasion and Season

YOU WILL DISCOVER HOW to prepare easy and delectable dog food recipes in this chapter for breakfast, lunch, dinner, snacks, treats, holidays, and other special occasions. Additionally, you will discover how to modify recipes for homemade dog food to your dog's specifications by experimenting with tastes, ingredients, and cooking methods. Additionally, you will learn how to adjust and change your dog food recipes based on factors like breed, size, age, activity level, and health.

How to Make Simple and Delicious Dog Food Recipes for Breakfast, Lunch, and Dinner

Breakfast, lunch, and dinner are among the times and seasons when you can prepare your own homemade dog food recipes. The three primary meals of the day—breakfast, lunch, and dinner—offer your dog the vital calories and nourishment they require to carry out their daily tasks and activities. You have more chances to form a stronger link and to show your dog how much you care and love them at breakfast, lunch, and dinner. To provide your dog the finest nutrition and food delight possible, you should prepare your own homemade dog food recipes for breakfast, lunch, and dinner.

For producing easy and delectable dog food recipes for breakfast, lunch, and dinner, consider the following advice and ideas:

Provide comprehensive and well-balanced dog food recipes. By creating full and balanced dog food recipes, you may avoid or lessen obesity, malnutrition, excess, or imbalance in your dog as well as give them the right number and quality of calories and nutrients. By utilizing the right products and supplements and adhering to the suggestions and guidelines for your dog's calorie and nutrient requirements, you may create balanced and comprehensive dog food recipes. If you need any help or guidance creating full and well-balanced dog food recipes, you should also speak with your veterinarian or a canine nutritionist.

Provide easy-to-follow recipes for dog food. You may save time and money by creating straightforward dog food recipes that also guarantee that your dog's food is prepared, portioned, and served in a hygienic and correct manner. By utilizing the standard and common ingredients and supplements, as well as according to the directions and specifications for each recipe, you may simplify and ease the creation of your dog food recipes. Along with using the proper tools and equipment, you should also cook, portion, and serve your dog's food according to the recommended methods. Additionally, you should limit or stay away from complex and exotic foods and supplements, as well as elegant and elaborate recipes, as they might be hazardous, expensive, or unnecessary for your dog.

Make your recipes for dog food tasty and visually appealing. In addition to ensuring that your dog receives the most nutrients and pleasure from their food, you may enhance your dog's appetite, digestion, and satisfaction by creating enticing and tasty dog food recipes. You should use premium, fresh ingredients and supplements in your dog food recipes, as well as adhere to the recipe's directions and standards, to make them tasty and visually appealing. Along with following the advice and recommendations for improving the taste, texture, and appearance of your dog's food, you should also add to or change the flavors, textures, and forms of it. In addition, you should take into account your dog's dietary requirements and taste preferences. If you need help creating enticing and tasty dog food recipes, speak with a canine nutritionist or your veterinarian.

Here are a few examples of easy and delectable breakfast, lunch, and dinner dog food recipes:

Oatmeal and scrambled eggs for breakfast. This is a really basic and straightforward breakfast recipe that gives your dog vitamins, fiber, and protein. To prepare this dish, you'll need:

Two eggs

One-fourth cup water

One-fourth teaspoon turmeric

Half a cup of porridge

One cup water

One-third cup honey

In order to prepare this dish, you must:

Whisk the eggs, water, and turmeric in a small bowl until thoroughly blended.

In a small saucepan, combine the oats and water. Bring to a boil, then lower the heat and simmer, stirring regularly, until the oatmeal becomes soft and creamy, about 15 minutes.

Pour the egg mixture into a small skillet that has been lightly oiled over medium-high heat. Cook, stirring periodically, for about ten minutes, or until the eggs are set.

Whisk the honey in a small bowl until it becomes runny and smooth.

After dividing the oats and eggs into two equal portions, cover the porridge with honey.

Give your dog a portion, and keep the remaining portion in the freezer for up to six months or the refrigerator for up to three days when stored in an airtight container.

Rice and chicken for lunch. This is a tried-and-true lunch meal that gives your dog minerals, carbs, and protein. To prepare this dish, you'll need:

One pound of chicken breast, deboned and skinless

Quater of water

Two cups of rice, brown.

Parsley, chopped, 1/4 cup

In order to prepare this dish, you must:

Place the chicken and water in a large pot, bring to a boil, then lower the heat and simmer for about 20 minutes, or until the chicken is cooked through.

After taking the chicken out of the pot, shred it using two forks.

In the same pot, add the rice and bring the water to a boil. After that, lower the heat and simmer the rice for about 40 minutes, or until it is fluffy and soft.

Using a fork, fluff the rice and stir in the parsley.

Separate the chicken and rice into four equal portions; give your dog one portion and keep the remaining sections in the freezer for up to six months or in the refrigerator for up to three days, covered tightly with containers.

Beef and vegetable stew for dinner. This dish for hearty and flavorful meal will give your dog the protein, fat, and vitamins that they need. To prepare this dish, you'll need:

Lean ground beef, one pound

TWO TABLETS OF OIL

Two-cup beef broth

two cups water

Two carrots, sliced and peeled

Two potatoes, diced and peeled

One-fourth cup peas

1/4 of a cup corn

One-fourth teaspoon salt

One-fourth teaspoon pepper

In order to prepare this dish, you must:

Heat the oil in a big skillet over medium-high heat. Add the beef and cook, breaking it up with a spatula, for about 15 minutes, or until it's browned and cooked through. After removing any surplus fat, move the steak to a big pot.

In the same pot, add the beef broth, water, carrots, potatoes, peas, corn, salt, and pepper. Bring to a boil, then lower the heat and simmer for about 30 minutes, or until the veggies are tender.

Split the stew into four equal portions; give your dog one portion and keep the remaining portions in the freezer for up to six months or in the refrigerator for up to three days, covered tightly with containers.

You may provide your dog the best nutrition and mealtime satisfaction by making easy and delectable dog food recipes for breakfast, lunch, and supper, and by heeding these advice and trying these examples. In addition, there are numerous common and major health issues that can be prevented or treated to enhance the quality and length of a dog's life.

How to Make Special and Festive Dog Food Recipes for Holidays, Birthdays, and Celebrations

HOLIDAYS, BIRTHDAYS, and celebrations are a few of the times of year when you can prepare your own homemade dog food recipes. For your dog, holidays, birthdays, and celebrations are the most exciting and joyous occasions of the year, offering him or her the chance to unwind and enjoy himself. Celebrate your dog's birthday, holiday, or any special occasion to show them how much you love and appreciate them and to make them feel unique and content. Therefore, to give your dog the finest nutrition and food satisfaction possible, make your own homemade dog food recipes for special occasions like holidays, birthdays, and celebrations.

For creating unique and festive dog food recipes for occasions like holidays, birthdays, and festivities, consider the following advice and suggestions:

Make sure your dog food recipes are suited for the time of year and the situation. You may feed your dog the necessary calories and nutrients and prevent or lessen discomfort, stress, and disease by creating dog food recipes that are suited for the time of year and the situation. By utilizing the right ingredients and supplements and adhering to instructions for your dog's calorie and nutrient requirements, you may tailor your dog food recipes to the occasion and season. If you need any help or guidance on how to modify your dog food recipes to fit the occasion and season, you should also speak with your veterinarian or a canine nutritionist.

For the occasion and season, add distinctive and festive touches to your dog food recipes. By tailoring your dog food recipes to the occasion and season, you can provide your dog the extra calories and nutrients they need while also preventing or lessening any boredom, discontent, or jealously on their part. By utilizing the appropriate special and festive ingredients and supplements, as well as according to each recipe's instructions and recommendations, you can make your dog food recipes unique and festive for the occasion and season. Along with following the advice and recommendations for improving the taste, texture, and appearance of your dog's food, you should also add to or change the flavors, textures, and forms of it. In addition, you should take into account your dog's dietary requirements and food allergies or intolerances. If you need help or guidance on how to customize your dog food recipes to fit the occasion and season, speak with your veterinarian or a canine nutritionist.

The following are a few instances of unique and celebratory dog food recipes for events like birthdays and holidays:

Thanksgiving dinner is turkey and cranberries. This dish for a unique and festive holiday meal gives your dog antioxidants, carbs, and protein. To prepare this dish, you'll need:

One pound of cooked, shredded turkey

Two cups of brown rice, cooked.

Dried cranberries, 1/4 cup

Two tsp finely chopped parsley

One-fourth teaspoon salt

One-fourth teaspoon pepper

In order to prepare this dish, you must:

Combine the turkey, rice, cranberries, parsley, salt, and pepper in a big bowl and toss everything thoroughly.

Separate the mixture into four equal portions. Give your dog one portion and keep the remaining portions in the freezer for up to six months or in the refrigerator for up to three days, respectively, in airtight containers.

Peanut butter and banana cake for my birthday. This dish for a unique and festive birthday meal gives your dog potassium, fat, and protein. To prepare this dish, you'll need:

Whole wheat flour, one cup

Just one tsp baking soda

one-fourth cup peanut butter

One-fourth cup vegetable oil

one-third cup honey

One egg

one mashed, ripe banana

Regarding the icing:

one-fourth cup peanut butter

one-fourth cup plain yogurt

One-fourth cup of heavy cream

Concerning the décor:

1/4 cup of peanuts, chopped

One-fourth cup of banana slices

In order to prepare this dish, you must:

Grease a 9-inch round cake pan and preheat the oven to 350 degrees.

Mix the baking soda and flour together thoroughly in a big bowl.

Mix the peanut butter, oil, honey, and egg thoroughly in a medium-sized bowl.

Add the mashed banana and well stir.

Once a smooth batter formed, pour the wet components into the dry ingredients and whisk.

Evenly spread the batter after pouring it onto the cake pan that has been ready.

When a toothpick inserted in the center comes out clean, bake for 25 to 30 minutes.

Allow the cake to cool fully on a wire rack within the pan.

In order to create the frosting, thoroughly mix the yogurt and peanut butter in a small bowl.

After adding the whipped cream, thoroughly combine.

Carefully take the cake out of the pan and lay it on a sizable plate or tray to assemble.

Evenly cover the cake's edges and top with icing.

Arrange the sliced bananas around the edge of the cake and scatter the chopped peanuts on top of the cake.

Cut the cake into eight equal pieces. Give your dog a slice, and keep the remaining slices in the freezer for up to six months or in the refrigerator for up to three days in an airtight container.

Bites of spinach and salmon to celebrate. This meal is a unique and joyous way to celebrate and gives your dog iron, fat, and protein. To prepare this dish, you'll need:

One-fourth pound of flakes cooked salmon

1/4 cup chopped cooked spinach

1/4 cup of grated cheese

1/4 cup of bread crumbs

One egg

1/4 teaspoon of garlic powder

One-fourth teaspoon salt

One-fourth teaspoon pepper

In order to prepare this dish, you must:

Put parchment paper on a baking pan and preheat the oven to 375°F.

Toss the salmon, spinach, cheese, bread crumbs, egg, garlic powder, salt, and pepper in a big basin until everything is completely mixed.

Form the mixture into walnut-sized balls, about the size of your fingers, and arrange them with some space between them on the baking sheet that has been preheated.

Bake 15 to 20 minutes, until firm and brown.

Transfer the bites to a sizable plate or tray after allowing them to cool slightly on the baking sheet.

Give your dog one or two bits, and store the remaining bites in the freezer for up to six months, or in the refrigerator for up to three days in an airtight container.

You may develop unique and festive dog food recipes for holidays, birthdays, and celebrations, and provide your dog the finest nutrition and food satisfaction possible by heeding their advice and suggestions and attempting these sample recipes. Additionally, you may make your dog feel unique and content by expressing your love, respect, and appreciation for them.

How to Make Creative and Fun Dog Food Recipes for Summer, Winter, and Other Seasons

SUMMER, WINTER, AND other seasons are among the times and situations when you can prepare your own homemade dog food recipes. Your dog can experience and enjoy varied weather conditions, climates, and environments throughout the year by going on walks in the summer, going on safari, and going on other seasons. You can also use the summer, winter, and other seasons to be imaginative and playful with your dog and to ensure their comfort and happiness. To provide your dog the finest nutrition and satisfaction from their diet, you should prepare your own homemade dog food recipes for the summer, winter, and other seasons.

The following are some ideas and pointers for coming up with imaginative and enjoyable dog food recipes for the summer, winter, and other seasons:

Adapt and adjust your dog food recipes according to the current season. By tailoring your dog food recipes to the season, you can prevent or lessen your dog's discomfort, stress, or disease while also giving them the pertinent and important calories and nutrients they require. Using the right ingredients and supplements, along with according to suggestions and standards for your dog's calorie and nutrient requirements, will help you create dog food recipes that are both appropriate and suitable for the current season. When creating dog food recipes that are suited for the current season, you should also seek guidance from a canine nutritionist or your veterinarian.

Bring some creativity and excitement to your dog food recipes this season. By incorporating seasonal creativity and fun into your dog food recipes, you may provide your dog the extra calories and nutrition they deserve while also preventing or lessening boredom, discontent, and jealously. By using the imaginative and enjoyable products and supplements and adhering to the directions and recommendations provided for each recipe, you can make your dog food recipes interesting and innovative for the current season. Along with following the advice and recommendations for improving the taste, texture, and appearance of your dog's food, you should also add to or change the flavors, textures, and forms of it. In addition, you ought to take into consideration your dog's dietary requirements and food allergies or intolerances. If you need help coming up with innovative and seasonal dog food recipes, speak with your veterinarian or a canine nutritionist.

The following are some inventive and enjoyable dog food recipe ideas for the summer, winter, and other seasons:

Popsicles with berries and frozen yogurt for summer. This is a tasty and inventive summer meal that gives your dog antioxidants, calcium, and protein. To prepare this dish, you'll need:

A pair of basic yogurt cups

A quarter-cup honey

One cup of berries mixed together, including strawberries, raspberries, and blueberries

Twelve tiny paper cups

Twelve wooden sticks.

In order to prepare this dish, you must:

Puree the yogurt, honey, and berries in a blender until the mixture is creamy and smooth.

Fill the paper cups approximately three quarters of the way to the top with the mixture.

After putting a wooden stick in the middle of each cup, freeze them for four hours or until solid.

To serve, peel off the paper cups, and give one popsicle to your dog, and store the remaining popsicles in a freezer bag in the freezer for up to two months.

Pumpkin & Spice Cookies for Winter. This is a tasty and inventive winter meal that gives your dog beta-carotene, fiber, and spices. To prepare this dish, you'll need:

Whole wheat flour, two cups

A single tsp of baking powder

One-fourth teaspoon cinnamon

one-fourth teaspoon ginger

One-fourth teaspoon nutmeg

One-fourth teaspoon salt

Half a cup of pureed pumpkin

One-fourth cup vegetable oil

one-fourth cup water

Two tablespoons of sugar syrup

In order to prepare this dish, you must:

Adjust the oven temperature to 350°F and place parchment paper on a baking pan.

Combine the flour, baking powder, nutmeg, ginger, cinnamon, and salt in a big basin and whisk them thoroughly.

Mix the pumpkin, molasses, water, and oil in a medium-sized bowl until thoroughly blended.

Once a soft dough develops, pour the wet components into the dry ingredients and stir.

Roll out the dough to a thickness of about 1/4 inch on a lightly floured board. Using cookie cutters, cut out figures like stars, snowflakes, or bones.

Leaving room between each cookie, place the cookies on the baking sheet that has been prepared.

Bake until crisp and golden, 15 to 20 minutes.

After allowing the cookies to cool fully on the baking sheet, move them to a sizable plate or platter.

Give your dog one or two cookies, and keep the rest in the freezer for up to two months, or in the refrigerator for up to two weeks in an airtight container.

Other seasons: Spring: Muffins with carrots and parsley. This is a fun and inventive spring meal that gives your dog iron, chlorophyll, and vitamin A. To prepare this dish, you'll need:

Whole wheat flour, two cups

Two tsp powdered baking powder

One-fourth teaspoon salt

one cup of carrots, grated

Parsley, chopped, 1/4 cup

One-fourth cup vegetable oil

A quarter-cup honey

two eggs

one-third cup milk

In order to prepare this dish, you must:

Grease a twelve-cup muffin tin and preheat the oven to 375°F.

Mix together the flour, baking powder, and salt in a big bowl until thoroughly blended.

Toss the carrot and parsley together in a medium-sized basin until thoroughly mixed.

Whisk together the eggs, milk, honey, and oil in a small bowl until thoroughly blended.

Add the carrot and parsley combination and thoroughly combine.

About three-quarters of the way full, spoon the batter into the muffin cups that have been prepped.

When a toothpick inserted in the center comes out clean, bake for 20 to 25 minutes.

After allowing the muffins to cool slightly in the pan, move them to a wire rack to finish cooling.

Give your dog one muffin at a time, and keep the rest in the freezer for up to two months in the refrigerator for up to three days when stored in an airtight container.

Apple and peanut butter bars for fall. This is a tasty and imaginative fall meal that gives your dog potassium, protein, and fiber. To prepare this dish, you'll need:

Double-cupped rolled oats

one-fourth cup peanut butter

One-fourth cup apple sauce

A quarter-cup honey

One-fourth teaspoon cinnamon

One-fourth teaspoon salt

one-fourth cup chopped apple

In order to prepare this dish, you must:

Heat the oven to 350°F and place parchment paper inside a 9 by 9-inch baking pan.

The oats, peanut butter, apple sauce, honey, cinnamon, and salt should all be thoroughly mixed together in a big bowl.

Add the chopped apple and well mix.

Using a spatula to flatten the surface, press the mixture firmly and evenly into the baking pan that has been prepared.

Bake for twenty to thirty minutes, or until firm and brown.

After allowing the bars to cool fully in the pan, cut them into 16 equal pieces.

Give your dog one piece, and keep the remaining portions in the freezer for up to two months or the refrigerator for up to one week in an airtight container.

You may produce tasty and imaginative dog food recipes for summer, winter, and other seasons and provide your dog the finest nutrition and food delight by heeding these advice and suggestions and experimenting with these samples. Making your dog feel comfortable and content is another way to be creative and enjoyable with them.

Chapter 5

The Secrets of Dog Treats and Snacks

THE SECRETS OF DOG treats and snacks are revealed in this chapter. You will discover how to produce nutritious and delectable treats and snacks for your dog, select the best commercial treats and snacks for your dog, and use treats and snacks for your dog sensibly and successfully.

The additional and infrequent foods you offer your dog in addition to their normal meals are known as dog treats and snacks. Dog snacks and treats can offer your dog a number of advantages, including:

Rewarding your dog when he performs well or reaches a goal; this serves to reinforce positive reinforcement training.

Motivating your dog to acquire new abilities, instructions, or tricks, and boosting their mental stimulation and enrichment.

Strengthening your bond and connection with your dog, as well as demonstrating your love and affection for them.

Enhancing your dog's dental health and hygiene while also satisfying their inclination to chew and bite.

Providing your dog with more calories and nutrients in their food, as well as treating or avoiding specific illnesses or ailments.

Dog treats and snacks, however, can also come with some risks and difficulties, like:

If administered excessively or incorrectly, leading to your dog's obesity, diabetes, or other health issues.

Making your dog's food allergies, intolerances, or sensitivities worse if it contains cheap, dangerous, or contaminated ingredients or additives.

Causing your dog to develop behavioral issues, including stealing, guarding food, or begging, if fed irregularly or carelessly.

Confusing or diverting your dog, and interfering with their learning or training, if provided at the improper time or place.

To give your dog the most nutrition and enjoyment from their food, you should manufacture or select your dog treats and snacks thoughtfully and sensibly, and utilize them effectively and ethically.

The following are some pointers and recommendations for selecting, preparing, and utilizing dog treats and snacks:

Make your own dog treats and snacks, or buy some nice, healthful options. In addition to giving your dog the ideal and balanced quantity and quality of calories and nutrients, you may prevent or lessen any harm or discomfort for your dog by making or selecting nutritious and delectable dog treats and snacks. The following guidelines should help you create or select delicious, nutritious dog treats and snacks for your pet:

In place of or reduce the use of artificial or synthetic substances, such as preservatives, colors, flavors, sweeteners, or fillers, use natural and healthful ingredients, such as meat, poultry, fish, eggs, dairy products, fruits, vegetables, grains, nuts, seeds, and herbs.

Use clean, fresh ingredients whenever possible. Steer clear of or use sparingly of any ruined or contaminated foods, such as those that have been exposed to chemicals, pesticides, or toxins, or that are moldy, rotting, or expired.

Employ suitable and secure components, and stay away from or restrict unsuitable or dangerous substances, such chocolate, raisins, grapes, onions, garlic, macadamia nuts, xylitol, alcohol, or foods that are too big, too little, too hard, or too sharp for your dog.

To guarantee that your dog receives a balanced and diversified intake of calories and nutrients, as well as to prevent or lessen any boredom, dissatisfaction, or allergy, use a variety of distinct components and avoid or restrict repetitive or boring ingredients.

To guarantee that your dog receives the appropriate and proper amount and quality of calories and nutrients that they need, as well as to prevent or lessen any obesity, malnutrition, deficiency, excess, or imbalance, use the right amount and proportion of ingredients and avoid or limit the wrong amount or proportion of ingredients.

Treats and snacks for dogs should be used sensibly and successfully. In addition to giving your dog the most advantages and enjoyment from their diet, using dog treats and snacks properly and responsibly can help prevent or lessen any problems or concerns that may develop from incorrect or irresponsible usage of dog treats and snacks. The following rules should help you use dog treats and snacks for your dog in an efficient and responsible manner:

Treats and snacks for dogs should be used in addition to regular meals, never as a replacement. Give your dog the essential calories and nutrients from regular meals, as well as any additional or infrequent calories and nutrients from treats and snacks.

Treats and snacks for dogs should be used as rewards rather than bribes for their good behavior, performance, or accomplishments. You should also provide your dog the fair and transparent expectations and guidelines they require from you, along with the positive reinforcement they need from their treats and snacks.

For your dog's learning, training, or enrichment, use dog treats and snacks as a motivator rather than a diversion. Give your dog the appropriate and timely stimulation and feedback they require from their treats and snacks, as well as the appropriate and challenging tasks and activities they require from you.

Treats and snacks for dogs should strengthen your dog's bond with you rather than act as a barrier to it. Give your dog the attention and love they require from you as well as the respect and trust they require from them.

Here are some examples of delectable and healthful dog treats and snacks that you may prepare yourself or choose out for your pet:

Homemade snacks and treats for dogs. Treats and snacks for dogs that you prepare yourself using your own materials, recipes, and techniques are referred to as homemade treats and snacks. You may create and customize homemade dog treats and snacks to fit your dog's needs and preferences, as well as have control and flexibility over the quantity and quality of your dog's treats and snacks. In addition to offering your dog the joy and fulfillment of creating their own treats and snacks, homemade dog treats and snacks can also allow you to express your love and care for your pet. The following are some examples of homemade dog snacks and treats that you can prepare for your canine companion:

Oatmeal with Peanut Butter Balls. These are easy-to-make snacks that are high in fiber, fat, and protein for your dog. What you'll need to prepare these goodies is:

Rolling oats, one cup

Two-thirds cup peanut butter

A quarter-cup honey

In order to prepare these goodies, you must:

Combine the oats, peanut butter, and honey in a big bowl and toss until thoroughly mixed.

Roll the mixture into marble-sized balls and arrange on a baking sheet covered with parchment paper.

Put the balls in the fridge to firm up, preferably for at least an hour.

Give your dog one or two balls at a time, and keep the rest in the freezer for up to two months in the refrigerator for up to one week in an airtight container.

Strips of cheese and chicken. These crunchy, cheese-flavored dog treats give your dog calcium, phosphorus, and protein. What you'll need to prepare these goodies is:

One cup of cooked, shredded chicken

One cup of cheese, grated

one-fourth cup water

Whole wheat flour, two cups

A single tsp of baking powder

In order to prepare these goodies, you must:

Heat the oven to 375°F and lightly coat a baking sheet with oil.

Place the chicken, cheese, and water in a small saucepan. Bring to a boil, then lower the heat and simmer for approximately ten minutes, stirring from time to time, until the cheese has melted.

Mix the flour and baking powder together in a big bowl until thoroughly blended.

When a stiff dough forms, add the chicken and cheese combination to the flour mixture and stir.

Roll out the dough to approximately 1/8 inch thick on a gently floured surface. Using a pizza cutter, cut the dough into strips that are about 1 inch wide and 4 inches long.

Leaving room between each strip, place the strips on the baking sheet that has been prepared.

Bake until crisp and golden, 15 to 20 minutes.

After allowing the strips to cool fully on the baking sheet, move them to a sizable plate or tray.

Give your dog one or two pieces at a time, and keep the remaining strips in the freezer for up to two months or the refrigerator for up to one week in an airtight container.

Apple and Carrot Muffins. These are fruity, moist dog treats that are high in antioxidants, fiber, and vitamin A. What you'll need to prepare these goodies is:

One cup of carrots, grated

One cup of apple grated
One-fourth cup vegetable oil
A quarter-cup honey
two eggs
Whole wheat flour, two cups
Just one tsp baking soda
One-fourth teaspoon cinnamon
In order to prepare these goodies, you must:
Grease a twelve-cup muffin tin and preheat the oven to 375°F.

Combine the carrot, apple, oil, honey, and eggs in a big bowl and whisk them well.

Mix the flour, baking soda, and cinnamon together in a medium-sized bowl.

When a smooth batter formed, add the dry ingredients to the wet ones and whisk.

About three-quarters of the way full, spoon the batter into the muffin cups that have been prepped.

When a toothpick inserted in the center comes out clean, bake for 20 to 25 minutes.

How to Make Healthy and Tasty Dog Treats and Snacks for Training, Rewarding, and Spoiling Your Dog

TREATS AND NIBBLES are a good idea if you want to train, reward, or otherwise spoil your dog. Your dog can gain a lot from being trained, pampered, or rewarded, including:

Enhancing your dog's conduct, output, or accomplishments and reiterating training with positive reinforcement.

Boosting your dog's self-esteem, drive, or contentment as well as their cerebral stimulation and enrichment.

Enhancing your interaction and communication with your dog, as well as fortifying your bond and demonstrating your love and affection for them.

Not every snack or treat, though, is helpful or appropriate for teaching, rewarding, or lavishing your dog. Certain foods and treats might be harmful, unappealing, or inappropriate for your dog, which could hurt or irritate them. To give your dog the finest nutrition and enjoyment from their diet, you should prepare your own nutritious and delectable treats and snacks for teaching, rewarding, or indulging them.

Here are some ideas and pointers for creating delectable and nutritious snacks and treats for your dog's training, rewards, or pampering:

Make your snacks and treats bite-sized and compact. Your dog will be less likely to choke, gag, or swallow treats and snacks if they are small and bite-sized, and they will be able to consume them more rapidly and effortlessly. You should use the right tools, like cookie cutters, molds, or knives, and adhere to the directions and specifications for each recipe to create bite-sized delights and snacks. Large, hard, or sticky treats and snacks—like bones, rawhides, or candies—that can be difficult or risky for your dog to consume should also be avoided or limited.

Reduce the amount of fat and calories in your desserts and snacks. Treats and snacks that are low in calories and fat will help your dog avoid obesity, diabetes, and other health issues while still allowing them to enjoy them without gaining too much weight or changing their regular diet. By using the right ingredients and supplements—such as lean meat, poultry, fish, eggs, dairy products, fruits, vegetables, grains, nuts, seeds, and herbs—and by adhering to the guidelines and recommendations for your dog's calorie and fat requirements, you can create treats and snacks that are low in calories and fat. Treats and snacks high in calories or fat, including cheese, bacon, butter, or oil, should also be avoided or consumed in moderation as they may be unneeded, costly, or detrimental to your dog.

Make sure your snacks and desserts are flavorful and full in protein. Your dog's appetite, digestion, and level of satisfaction will all be enhanced by giving them treats and snacks that are high in flavor and protein. They will also be able to consume them with excitement and joy. Using the right ingredients and supplements—meat, poultry, fish, eggs, dairy products, fruits, vegetables, grains, nuts, seeds, and herbs—as well as adhering to the directions and recommendations for each dish can help you create treats and snacks that are high in protein and flavor. Along with following the advice and recommendations for improving the flavor, texture, and look of your treats and snacks, you should also add to or change the flavors, textures, and forms of your creations. In addition, you should take into account your dog's dietary requirements and taste preferences. If you need help or guidance on how to prepare treats and snacks that are high in flavor and protein, speak with your veterinarian or a canine nutritionist.

Here are some ideas of delectable and healthful snacks and treats you may create for your dog as a training aid, reward, or spoiler:

Liver and Oat Cookies for training. These are flavorful, crunchy treats that give your dog fiber, iron, and protein. What you'll need to prepare these goodies is:

1/4 pound of chopped beef liver

One cup water

Rolling oats, one cup

One-fourth cup whole wheat flour

one-fourth teaspoon powdered garlic

One-fourth teaspoon salt

In order to prepare these goodies, you must:

Adjust the oven temperature to 350°F and place parchment paper on a baking pan.

Place the liver and water in a small saucepan, bring to a boil, then lower the heat and simmer for approximately 15 minutes, or until the liver is tender.

After draining the liver, set aside the broth.

Puree the liver in a food processor or blender until it's smooth.

Combine the oats, flour, salt, and garlic powder in a big bowl and toss until thoroughly mixed.

Stir in 1/4 cup of the broth and the liver purée.

Using a fork, gently flatten the dough droplets after placing them on the baking sheet that has been ready.

Bake until crisp and golden, 15 to 20 minutes.

After allowing the cookies to cool fully on the baking sheet, move them to a sizable plate or platter.

Give your dog one or two cookies, and keep the rest in the freezer for up to two months, or in the refrigerator for up to one week in an airtight container.

Carrot and peanut butter bites are rewarding. These are protein, fat, and vitamin A-rich soft and sweet snacks for your dog. What you'll need to prepare these goodies is:

two-thirds cup peanut butter

A quarter-cup honey

one cup of carrots, grated

one-fourth cup coconut flour

In order to prepare these goodies, you must:

Microwave the honey and peanut butter in a big bowl for about 30 seconds, or until smooth and melted, stirring every now and again.

Mix thoroughly after adding the coconut flour and carrot.

Roll the mixture into marble-sized balls and arrange on a baking sheet covered with parchment paper.

Put the balls in the fridge to firm up, preferably for at least an hour.

Give your dog one or two balls at a time, and keep the rest in the freezer for up to two months in the refrigerator for up to one week in an airtight container.

Warning: This recipe contains spoilers. These are cheesy, moist treats that give your dog phosphorus, calcium, and protein. What you'll need to prepare these goodies is:

Four bacon pieces, diced

One cup of cheese, grated

one-fourth cup water

Whole wheat flour, two cups

A single tsp of baking powder

In order to prepare these goodies, you must:

Grease a twelve-cup muffin tin and preheat the oven to 375°F.

Cook the bacon in a small skillet over medium-high heat, tossing regularly, until it becomes crisp, about 10 minutes. After removing any excess fat, move the bacon to a small bowl.

Add the cheese and water to a small saucepan, bring to a boil, then lower the heat and simmer, stirring occasionally, until the cheese is melted, about 10 minutes.

Mix the flour and baking powder together in a big bowl until thoroughly blended.

Stir in the bacon and cheese mixture until a stiff dough forms.

About three-quarters of the way full, spoon the dough into the muffin cups that have been prepared.

Bake for twenty to twenty-five minutes, until firm and brown.

After allowing the muffins to cool slightly in the pan, move them to a wire rack to finish cooling.

Give your dog one muffin at a time, and keep the rest in the freezer for up to two months in the refrigerator for up to three days when stored in an airtight container.

You may give your dog the finest nutrition and enjoyment from their diet by making nutritious and delicious treats and snacks for training, rewarding, or spoiling them. Just follow these guidelines and give these examples a try. Additionally, you can foster a closer link with your dog and demonstrate your love and affection for them, as well as enhance your dog's motivation, self-assurance, or contentment.

Chapter 6

The Tips and Tricks of Dog Food Shopping and Budgeting

THE BEST AND FRESHEST ingredients and supplements for your dog's food can be found in this chapter, along with time and money-saving tips like buying in bulk, using coupons, and comparing prices, as well as how to budget for and keep track of your dog's food expenses and consumption.

The practical and crucial parts of creating your own homemade dog food and treats are shopping for dog food and creating a budget. These decisions can have an impact on your personal money, convenience, and the quantity and quality of your dog's food. Budgeting and dog food buying can also provide you a number of advantages, including:

Ensuring that your dog receives the best possible nutrition and care, treating or preventing many common and major health issues that plague dogs, and extending both the quality and quantity of their life.

Making your own homemade dog food and treats with the best and freshest ingredients and supplements that you can afford will save you money, time, and lessen your influence on the environment. Avoid or restrict the costly, low-quality, or wasteful commercial dog food and treats.

Making your own homemade dog food and treats with the ingredients and supplements that you want will allow you to express your love and creativity while also having fun and feeling satisfied. You can also customize and personalize your dog food and treats to fit your dog's needs and preferences.

But budgeting and dog food purchasing can also present some obstacles and problems, like:

Identifying and selecting the best ingredients and supplements for your dog's food, making sure they are safe, wholesome, and appropriate for your dog, as well as meeting their nutritional and energy needs, taste preferences, and any food allergies or intolerances.

locating and selecting the greatest offers and discounts on dog food, making sure they fit into your budget, offer the best value and quality for the money, and don't jeopardize the wellbeing or health of your pet.

Organizing and monitoring your dog's food costs and intake can help you make sure that they are sustainable, reasonable, and do not exceed your income or savings. They will also help you and your dog avoid stress or financial or dietary instability.

In order to provide your dog the most nutrition and satisfaction from their food and to give yourself the best financial and practical results from your dog food buying and budgeting, you should heed the advice and implement these tips and methods.

How to Shop for the Best and Freshest Ingredients and Supplements for Your Dog's Food

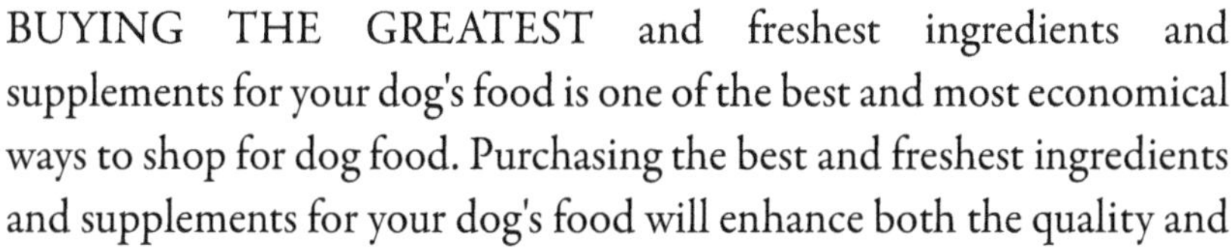

BUYING THE GREATEST and freshest ingredients and supplements for your dog's food is one of the best and most economical ways to shop for dog food. Purchasing the best and freshest ingredients and supplements for your dog's food will enhance both the quality and quantity of your dog's life while giving them the optimal and balanced nutrition and care they deserve. It can also prevent or treat many of the common and serious health issues that affect dogs.

The following are some pointers and recommendations for finding the greatest and freshest ingredients and additives for the food your dog eats:

Purchase from reliable sources and locations. The best and freshest ingredients and supplements for your dog's food can be found by going to the right stores and suppliers. You can also be sure that the ingredients are safe, fresh, and appropriate for your dog, and that they will satisfy all of their nutritional and calorie needs as well as their taste preferences and any food allergies or intolerances. You ought to purchase from reliable sources and locations, like:

Farmers' markets, both organic and local, offer a wide variety of locally grown, seasonal, and fresh produce, including fruits, vegetables, grains, nuts, seeds, and herbs. The produce is grown without the use of pesticides, chemicals, or toxins, and it is high in nutrients, minerals, antioxidants, and phytochemicals while being low in calories, fat, and sodium.

Fresh, lean, organic meat, poultry, fish, eggs, and dairy products that are raised without the use of hormones, antibiotics, or additives and are high in protein, iron, zinc, calcium, and omega-3 fatty acids but low in calories, fat, and cholesterol can be found in local and organic butcher shops.

LOCAL AND ORGANIC HEALTH food stores stock a variety of fresh, natural, and organic ingredients and supplements, including nut butter, yogurt, cheese, spices, herbs, oils, vinegars, honey, molasses, and supplements. These products are free of artificial or synthetic ingredients, including colors, flavors, sweeteners, and preservatives. They are also high in flavor, fat, and calories, and low in sodium, sugar, and additives.

Online pet food stores with a good reputation are a good place to find high-quality, fresh ingredients and supplements, like liver, kidney, heart, tripe, bone meal, kelp, brewer's yeast, probiotics, enzymes, vitamins, and minerals. These supplements are made especially for dogs and are high in nutrients, calories, and health benefits while being low in allergens, contaminants, and side effects.

Shop with the appropriate understanding and information. When you shop with the right knowledge and understanding, you can find the best and freshest ingredients and supplements for your dog's food. You can also make sure that these ingredients and supplements are safe, fresh, and appropriate for your dog, and that they meet their calorie and nutrient requirements as well as their taste preferences and any allergies or intolerances. When shopping, you should be well-informed and knowledgeable about things like:

Age, size, breed, activity level, and health issues can all have an impact on your dog's ability to grow, develop, and maintain immunity. These factors can also have an impact on your dog's need for calories and nutrients, as well as their taste preferences and any allergies or intolerances they may have. For help figuring out how many calories and nutrients your dog needs, as well as how to accommodate their taste preferences and any food allergies or intolerances, speak with your veterinarian or a canine nutritionist.

The nutrients and additives you use in your dog's diet can have an impact on its quantity and quality, as well as how well-nourished and enjoyable it is for them. For your dog's food, you should adhere to the directions and guidelines provided with each recipe, use only suitable and safe ingredients and supplements, and steer clear of or use them sparingly in combination with inappropriate or dangerous ingredients and supplements. You should also label your ingredients and supplements with the name, date, and source of the product or supplement, and follow the expiration dates or shelf lives of the ingredients and supplements that you use for your dog's food.

The tools and equipment that you use for your dog's food, which might affect the cooking and storage of your dog's food, and consequently the freshness and safety of your dog's food. You should follow the directions and rules for each recipe, and use the necessary and clean tools and equipment, such as knives, cutting boards, spoons, cups, scales, bowls, plates, trays, mats, pots, pans, ovens, microwaves, refrigerators, freezers, and containers, for your dog's food. You should also follow the recommendations and ideas for cooking, portioning, and serving your dog's food, and for storing, freezing, and thawing your dog's food.

How to Save Money and Time by Buying in Bulk, Using Coupons, and Comparing Prices

ONE OF THE TIPS AND tricks of dog food shopping and budgeting is to save money and time by buying in bulk, using coupons, and comparing prices. Saving money and time by buying in bulk, using coupons, and comparing prices can provide you with the best value and quality for your money, and ensure that you can afford and access the best and freshest ingredients and supplements for your dog's food, and that you do not compromise your dog's health or happiness.

Here are some of the tips and suggestions for saving money and effort by buying in bulk, using coupons, and comparing prices:

Buy in quantity. Buying in bulk can save you money and time, by allowing you to buy more of the ingredients and supplements that you need for your dog's food, at a reduced price per unit, and by reducing the frequency and trouble of your shopping excursions. You should buy in bulk, by following these criteria:

Buy the ingredients and supplements that you use frequently and regularly for your dog's food, such as meat, poultry, fish, eggs, dairy products, fruits, vegetables, grains, nuts, seeds, herbs, oils, vinegars, spices, honey, molasses, peanut butter, yogurt, cheese, and supplements, and avoid or limit the ingredients and supplements that you use rarely or occasionally for your dog's food, such as liver, kidney, heart, tripe, bone meal, kelp, brewer's yeast, probiotics, enzymes, vitamins, minerals, and supplements, as they may expire or spoil before you use them, or they may be unnecessary, expensive, or harmful for your dog.

Buy the ingredients and supplements that have a long shelf life and can be stored easily and conveniently for your dog's food, such as dried, canned, frozen, or vacuum-packed ingredients and supplements, and avoid or limit the ingredients and supplements that have a short shelf life and require special or careful storage for your dog's food, such as fresh, raw, or cooked ingredients and supplements, as they may lose their freshness, quality, or safety over time, or they may require more space, equipment, or energy for storage.

Buy the ingredients and supplements that are in season and on sale for your dog's food, such as fruits, vegetables, grains, nuts, seeds, and herbs, that are cheaper, fresher, and more abundant during certain times of the year, and avoid or limit the ingredients and supplements that are out of season and expensive for your dog's food, such as fruits, vegetables, grains, nuts, seeds, and herbs, that are scarce, costly, and of lower quality during other times of the year.

Apply coupons. By enabling you to purchase the necessary ingredients and supplements for your dog's food at a discounted or reduced price and by lowering the amount of money you spend on your shopping visits, using coupons can help you save money and time. When using coupons, make sure to adhere to these guidelines:

Coupons that offer a percentage off, a dollar off, a buy one get one free, or a free sample or trial are examples of valid and applicable coupons for the ingredients and supplements you need for your dog's food. Avoid or limit using coupons that are expired or irrelevant for the ingredients and supplements you need for your dog's food, such as those that offer a product or service that you do not need or want, or that have a minimum purchase amount or other restrictions that you cannot meet or comply with.

Utilize the coupons that you can find online, in newspapers, magazines, flyers, mailers, or from stores, manufacturers, or organizations for the ingredients and supplements you need for your dog's food. Avoid or limit the coupons that are unavailable or inaccessible for the ingredients and supplements you need for your dog's food, such as those that require payment, registration, collection, or redemption, or that require you to travel far or wait a long time.

For the ingredients and supplements you need for your dog's food, use the coupons that are valuable and beneficial, such as those that offer a sizable or substantial savings, can be combined or stacked with other coupons or offers, or can be used repeatedly or for multiple products. Avoid or use as few as possible the coupons that are useless or detrimental, such as those that offer a negligible or trivial saving, can only be used once or for a single product.

Examine costs. By enabling you to get the necessary ingredients and supplements for your dog's food at the lowest or best price and by cutting down on the time you spend looking for and making decisions during your shopping visits, pricing comparisons can help you save both money and time. You should use the following standards to compare prices:

Compare the costs of the ingredients and supplements you need for your dog's food from various locations and sources, such as reputable online pet food stores, local and organic farmers' markets, local and organic butcher shops, local and organic health food stores, and other establishments that sell the necessary ingredients and supplements. Then, select the location or source that meets your other requirements, such as freshness, quality, and safety, and offers the lowest or best price.

Examine the costs of various brands and varieties of the ingredients and supplements you need for your dog's food, including generic, store-brand, or name-brand; organic, natural, or conventional; and various flavors, textures, or shapes. Then, select the brand or variety that offers the best or lowest price for the ingredients and supplements you need for your dog's food, while also satisfying your other requirements, such as nutrition, taste, and suitability.

The costs of the ingredients and supplements you require for your dog's food should be compared between various units and quantities, such as pounds, ounces, grams, kilograms, liters, milliliters, cups, tablespoons, teaspoons, or pieces of ingredients and supplements; alternatively, you can compare the costs of single, double, triple, or multiple packs or containers of ingredients and supplements. Finally, select the unit or quantity that offers the best or lowest price per unit or quantity for the ingredients and supplements you require for your dog's food while also satisfying your other requirements, such as shelf life, storage, and eating.

You can save time and money by comparing prices, buying in bulk, using coupons, and getting the best value and quality for your money. You can also give your dog the freshest and best ingredients and supplements for their food by adhering to these tips and suggestions and trying these examples.

How to Plan and Track Your Dog's Food Expenses and Consumption

NOT ONLY ARE DOGS OUR best friends, but they are also our devoted family members and companions. We should give them the finest diet and care possible. But feeding your dog can also be very expensive and difficult to arrange. How much food is appropriate for your dog? Which food type ought should you purchase? How can you monitor the amount of food your dog eats and how much it costs? We'll address these concerns in this chapter along with offering some advice and resources to help you budget for and monitor your dog's food costs and intake.

How Much Food Is Appropriate for Your Dog?

Your dog's nutritional requirements are influenced by a number of variables, including his age, weight, breed, degree of activity, overall health, and the kind and caliber of food you are giving him. Generally speaking, you should either ask your veterinarian for help or adhere to the feeding recommendations found on the food container. These are simply approximations, though, and they might not meet your dog's specific demands. As a result, you should keep an eye on your dog's physical health and modify his food consumption as necessary. Using the Body Condition Score (BCS) method, which is a scale from 1 to 9 that shows how skinny or fat your dog is, is a useful way to achieve this. A score of 4 or 5 is regarded as optimum, but a score of 1 or 9 indicates that the person is either too thin or too overweight. Visit this link for additional details and BCS system examples: https://www.bing.com/search?q=dog+condition+body+score

Examine your dog's tummy, waist, and ribs to determine his BCS. Though barely visible, his ribs should be easily felt. When seen from above, he should have a noticeable waist, and when seen from the side, his abdomen should be slightly tucked in. You should give your dog more food or switch to a higher-calorie food if he is too lean. You should give your dog less food or switch to a lower-calorie diet if he is overweight. Additionally, you want to take your dog's activity level into account and modify his food intake appropriately. For instance, your dog can require more food than a couch potato if he plays sports or is extremely active. On the other hand, your dog can require less food than a typical dog if he is sedentary or has a medical condition that restricts his activities.

Which Food Should You Purchase?

The market is flooded with dog food brands and varieties, so it might be difficult to choose the best for your pooch. Dog food comes in three main varieties: wet, dry, and raw. Before choosing one, you should carefully consider the benefits and drawbacks of each type. When selecting a dog food variety, keep the following things in mind:

Nutrition: The food's nutritional content should be taken into account above anything else. To make sure the food has the minimal amounts of nutrients dogs require, search for one that satisfies the Association of American Feed Control Officials (AAFCO) requirements. Since dogs are carnivores and fare best on a diet high in meat, you should also seek for a food that has a low percentage of carbohydrates and a high percentage of protein. Foods with artificial flavors, colors, preservatives, or fillers should be avoided because they may cause allergies in your dog or other health issues. Aside from the freshness of the food, you should also check its expiration date because spoilt or stale food might make your dog sick.

Cost: The price of the food is an additional consideration. In general, the most expensive food is wet food, raw food is somewhere in between, and dry food is the least expensive. But the quantity and quality of the food also affect the price. To ascertain the actual cost of the food, you should evaluate the price per pound or kilogram of the food in addition to the quantity and frequency of feedings. The cost of preparation and storage should also be taken into account, since certain foods may need to be cooked or refrigerated. Look for ways to cut costs on dog food, such purchasing in bulk, using coupons, or signing up for loyalty clubs.

Preference: Your dog's preferences are the last thing to take into account. Certain dogs may have dietary preferences, allergies, or sensitivity to particular foods. It is important to watch how your dog responds to the meal in terms of his energy, appetite, coat, feces, and demeanor. You've found a nice food for your dog if he enjoys it and doesn't seem uncomfortable or sick. You should give your dog an alternative food if they express distaste for it or exhibit symptoms of illness. To prevent upset stomachs, you should gradually introduce new meals to your dog by combining them with the old diet and increasing the percentage over a few days.

How Can You Monitor the Amount of Food Your Dog Eats and Spends?

You can make sure that your dog is receiving the proper quantity and quality of food by monitoring both their food intake and budget. You can also use this information to manage your expenditures and prevent overspending. There are numerous methods for monitoring your dog's food consumption and spending, including:

Using a measuring cup or scale: Make sure you measure out the precise amount of food your dog is eating and adhere to the feeding recommendations on the food packaging or the advice of your veterinarian. Additionally, you want to keep track of how much food you are giving your dog and contrast it with his weight and BCS. In this manner, you may avoid overfeeding or underfeeding your dog and modify his food consumption as necessary.

Using a food diary or spreadsheet: You should keep track of the kind, brand, and price of the dog food you buy, along with the date and location of purchase, by keeping a food diary or spreadsheet. Along with the date and time of feeding, you should also note how much food you are giving your dog. In this manner, you can keep an eye on your dog's food expenditures and consumption and adjust your purchasing and budget accordingly.

Using an app or website: You may monitor your dog's food consumption and spending by using an app or website. Features like food calculators, food databases, meal reviews, food delivery, food coupons, and more are available on a plethora of applications and websites. These websites and apps include, for instance:

Dog Food Advisor: This website offers thorough, objective evaluations and ratings of dog food brands and products according to their nutritional value, recall history, and ingredients. This website allows you to search for the finest dog food discounts and bargains as well as compare and select the best food for your dog. You can also subscribe to email notifications and alerts on news and recalls pertaining to dog food. This website can be viewed at https://www.dogfoodadvisor.com/.

With the Petnet SmartFeeder, an app and gadget on your smartphone, you may use the appropriate amount and timing of food to be automatically fed to your dog. Based on your dog's age, weight, breed, and activity level, you may adjust his feeding schedule and portion amount using this app and gadget. Additionally, you can order extra food for your dog as needed by using this app and gadget to track their food intake and inventory. Notifications and alerts regarding your dog's health and feeding status are also available to you. Visit this link to learn more and get the app and gadget: https://www.petnet.io/smartfeeder

PetBudget: This program assists you in organizing and monitoring the costs associated with your dog, such as food, veterinary care, grooming, toys, and more. With the help of this software, you can record and organize your dog's spending as well as make a monthly budget. With the help of this app, you can also see statistics and charts that show the trends and spending patterns of your dog as well as obtain advice on how to reduce the costs associated with keeping them. This app is available for download at https://www.petbudget.app.

These are a few methods for organizing and monitoring the cost and intake of food for your dog. You can manage your finances and save money by using these tools and advice to make sure your dog is receiving the finest care and nourishment that he deserves.

Chapter 7

How to Answer the Most Common and Important Questions About Homemade Dog Food

AMONG DOG OWNERS AND specialists, homemade dog food is a hotly debated topic. While some people strongly advise against it, others swear by it. When it comes to homemade dog food, a lot of queries and worries come up, like:

Is homemade dog food superior to store-bought dog food?

What advantages and disadvantages come with homemade dog food?

How can I prepare a comprehensive, well-balanced homemade dog food?

How much should your dog be fed in homemade dog food?

How should homemade dog food be prepared and stored?

How can you transition your dog from store-bought to homemade dog food?

We will attempt to address these queries in this chapter and offer a few sources and recommendations for more details and direction. We sincerely hope that this chapter will assist you in choosing homemade dog food for your dog in a sensible and knowledgeable manner.

Is homemade dog food superior to store-bought dog food?

This topic lacks a solid response because both homemade and store-bought dog food have advantages and disadvantages. Both commercial and homemade dog food's suitability and quality are determined by a number of variables, including the ingredients, the recipe, the method, the storage, the amount and frequency of feedings, the age, weight, breed, activity level, and health of the dog as well as the owner's time, resources, and budget.

Compared to commercial dog food, homemade dog food is typically thought to be fresher, more natural, and more personalized. You may customize homemade dog food to your dog's requirements and tastes by selecting the ingredients, amounts, and supplements. Additionally, homemade dog food can assist you in avoiding certain chemicals, additives, or allergies that can be found in some commercial dog food. Additionally, homemade dog food can be less expensive than store-bought dog food, particularly if you use organic, seasonal, or local products and purchase in bulk or during a discount.

However, there are disadvantages and difficulties with making dog food at home. Compared to commercial dog food, homemade dog food needs more time, work, and expertise. It might take a lot of time and energy to plan, prepare, shop, make, and store homemade dog food on a regular basis. It might be challenging and perplexing to make sure homemade dog food satisfies your dog's nutritional needs and standards. For your dog to be as healthy and perform as possible, you must balance the macronutrients (protein, fat, and carbohydrates), the micronutrients (vitamins and minerals), and the supplements (calcium, omega-3 fatty acids, and probiotics). Additionally, you must keep an eye on your dog's weight, body type, and overall health and modify his homemade dog food as necessary. If not prepared or kept correctly, homemade dog food might potentially present some health dangers for your dog, such as bacterial contamination, nutrient excess, or deficiency.

On the other hand, commercial dog food is typically thought to be more controlled, consistent, and convenient than homemade dog food. You can feed your dog with the least amount of trouble and fuss by using commercial dog food. All you have to do is purchase commercial dog food, keep it, and feed it in accordance with the directions on the packaging or the guidance of your veterinarian. Because commercial dog food is developed and evaluated by professionals, it also guarantees that your dog will receive the proper and balanced nutrients. The Association of American Feed Control Officials (AAFCO) sets rules and criteria for commercial dog food, which ensures that the food meets the minimal nutrient requirements for dogs. In addition, commercial dog food comes in a range of tastes and alternatives for your dog, including dry, wet, tinned, frozen, dehydrated, or raw food, as well as various formulae for various sizes, breeds, life stages, or medical concerns.

Commercial dog food does, however, have certain restrictions and disadvantages. Because commercial dog food is mass-produced and standardized, it might not be suitable for your dog's specific needs or preferences. Additionally, certain elements found in commercial dog food may be harmful or superfluous for your dog, such as artificial flavors, colors, preservatives, or fillers; alternatively, low-quality or by-product meats, grains, or vegetables may be used. Additionally, homemade dog food may be less affordable than commercial dog food, particularly if you purchase premium or specialist brands or products.

Thus, the question of whether homemade dog food is superior to store-bought dog food will ultimately rely on your own preferences and the circumstances around your dog. You should consider the advantages and disadvantages of both commercial and homemade dog food, and seek guidance from your veterinarian. To get the best of both worlds, you can also feed your dog a combination of homemade and commercial dog food, or alternate between the two. Feeding your dog a complete, well-balanced, and high-quality cuisine that fulfills his taste buds and meets his nutritional demands is crucial.

How to Find and Use the Most Reliable and Helpful Sources of Information and Advice on Homemade Dog Food

PREPARING HOMEMADE dog food for your pet can be a fun and fulfilling endeavor, but it can also be intimidating and perplexing. Numerous online resources, including books, blogs, podcasts, videos, periodicals, newsletters, forums, organizations, and social media, are available for information and guidance about making homemade dog food. But not every source is trustworthy and beneficial—some could even be detrimental or deceptive. How can you locate and utilize the most trustworthy and beneficial sources of knowledge and guidance on homemade dog food? Here are some guidelines and pointers to assist you:

Examine the credentials and reputation of the source: You want to find reliable, competent experts—such as veterinarians, nutritionists, or animal scientists—who have the necessary expertise, education, and experience in the field of canine nutrition and health—who have written, edited, or otherwise endorsed the material. In the dog community, you should also seek out credible and well-known sources, such as those with awards, ratings, reviews, testimonials, or references. Sources that are authored, edited, or supported by unreliable, unidentified people or groups should be avoided as they might be biased, have hidden objectives, or be involved in conflicts of interest such as propagating false information, selling goods, or advancing political causes.

Verify the information's quality and correctness by looking for reliable sources that offer facts, statistics, data, studies, and research that are supported by scientific evidence, peer-reviewed literature, professional standards, or other reliable sources. Additionally, you should search for sources that follow proper grammar, spelling, and formatting, are easy to read, understand, and follow, and offer information that is clear, succinct, and consistent. Avoid information from sources that lack scientific backing, peer-reviewed literature, professional standards, or are based on opinions, anecdotes, rumors, or low-quality or erroneous information based on one's own experiences, beliefs, or preferences. Additionally, you should stay away from sites that utilize poor grammar, spelling, or formatting, are difficult to read, comprehend, or follow, or that provide information in an ambiguous, confusing, or contradictory manner.

Verify the information's relevancy and currency by looking for sources that offer up-to-date, pertinent information that is frequently updated, changed, or validated and that take into account any new advances, trends, or discoveries in the field of canine nutrition and health. Additionally, search for resources that address the unique needs of your dog, including age, weight, breed, activity level, health condition, or preference, and that offer doable and reasonable solutions, advice, or ideas for preparing homemade dog food. Sources that offer out-of-date or irrelevant material, are not frequently updated, changed, or confirmed, or do not accurately reflect the most recent advancements, trends, or discoveries in the field of dog nutrition and health should all be avoided. Additionally, steer clear of any sources that offer advice or techniques for creating homemade dog food that is unrealistic or impractical, that are not unique to the needs of your dog, or that are irrelevant or inapplicable.

Several trustworthy and beneficial resources offering guidance and information on making dog food at home include:

The authors of The Ultimate Guide to Homemade Dog Food, Dr. Karen Becker, an animal nutritionist and holistic veterinarian, and Beth Taylor, a dog trainer and nutrition consultant, have over thirty years of combined experience preparing homemade dog food for dogs of various breeds, ages, and health issues. This book offers more than fifty recipes for balanced and full homemade dog food that are supported by professional standards, empirical data, and real-world experience. It also offers thorough and exhaustive information on the advantages, hazards, and preparation techniques of homemade dog food. Here is where you can buy this book and find out more information: https://www.bing.com/search?The definitive guide to homemade dog food

Author Linda P. Case has over 25 years of experience teaching, researching, and writing about dog nutrition and health. Her book, Dog Food Logic: Making Smart Decisions for Your Dog in an Age of Too Many Choices, is authored by Case. This book offers unbiased and critical analysis of the benefits and drawbacks of various dog food varieties, including homemade dog food, along with the knowledge and abilities needed to assess and contrast dog food labels, ingredients, and products that are supported by scientific data, peer-reviewed literature, and industry standards. Here is where you can buy this book and find out more information: https://www.bing.com/search?q=food+logic+dog

Balance IT: Based on your dog's individual needs and tastes as well as the items you have on hand, this website and app assists you in creating full and well-balanced homemade dog food recipes. Using this website and app, you can enter your dog's details—such as age, weight, breed, activity level, health condition, or preference—as well as the ingredients you'd like to use, like meat, vegetables, grains, or supplements, to receive a personalized recipe that satisfies your dog's nutritional needs and is based on professional standards, scientific evidence, and advice from experts. Additionally, you may use this website and app to order the vitamins, minerals, and amino acids—among other supplements—that you need for your homemade dog food. These supplements are created and tested by nutritionists and veterinarians. Here is the link to this website and app, where you can get additional details: https://secure.balanceit.com/

These are a few pointers and standards to assist you in locating and utilizing the most trustworthy and beneficial sources of knowledge and guidance regarding homemade dog food. You can make sure that you are getting the greatest guidance and information for preparing homemade dog food for your dog by adhering to these guidelines and standards. This will also help you avoid the pitfalls and issues that may result from using untrustworthy and ineffective sources.

How to Connect and Share with Other Dog Owners and Experts Who Make Homemade Dog Food

IT CAN BE A LONELY and alienating experience to make homemade dog food, especially if you have no one with whom to share your successes and setbacks. On the other hand, you are not alone in your endeavor to prepare homemade dog food. There are plenty of other dog lovers and specialists out there who are happy to connect and share their knowledge about making homemade dog food with you. How can you interact and exchange information with other dog owners and dog food specialists who prepare homemade dog food? The following channels and methods can assist you:

Join online forums and groups: You can interact and communicate with other dog owners and experts who make homemade dog food by joining online forums and groups devoted to the topic. There, you can exchange knowledge, experiences, tales, questions, and answers as well as recipes, advice, tips, and suggestions for making homemade dog food. Along with making new friends or contacts who share your enthusiasm and interest in homemade dog food, you can also get support, encouragement, criticism, and inspiration from other dog owners and professionals who make dog food. Several online forums and groups that focus on making homemade dog chow include the following:

Dog Food Forum: This is an online forum where people can talk and discuss dog food-related subjects, such as homemade dog food. This online forum allows you to post and read topics about homemade dog food, including its costs, ingredients, procedures, advantages, and drawbacks. You can also obtain responses and advice from experts who also prepare homemade dog food as well as other dog owners. Additionally, you can search and browse the archives of this online forum's resources, which include books, podcasts, videos, blogs, articles, and articles about making homemade dog food. Visit this website to join the online discussion and obtain additional information: https://www.dogfoodforum.com/

The Facebook group Homemade Dog Food Recipes is devoted to sharing recipes for homemade dog food. This online group allows you to share and like photographs and videos of recipes for homemade dog food, as well as receive comments, shares, and likes from other dog owners and professionals in the field. Additionally, you can utilize this online group to seek advice or comments from other dog owners and professionals who prepare homemade dog food, as well as to ask and answer questions about homemade dog food recipes, including those regarding ingredients, amounts, supplements, and processing. Here's where you can join the group and get more details: https://www.facebook.com/groups/homemadedogfoodrecipes

Attend offline events and activities: You can meet and socialize with other dog owners and professionals who make homemade dog food at offline events and activities. There, you can exchange information, stories, experiences, questions, answers, recipes, tips, and suggestions about making homemade dog food. Along with making new friends or contacts who share your enthusiasm and interest in homemade dog food, you can also get support, encouragement, criticism, and inspiration from other dog owners and professionals who make dog food. The following are a few instances of offline occasions and pursuits linked to homemade dog food:

Homemade Dog Food Workshop: Taught by a veterinarian or nutritionist with expertise in homemade dog food, this is an offline workshop that teaches you how to prepare homemade dog food for your dog. With the help of the instructor and other participants, you may utilize this offline workshop to understand the fundamentals and principles of creating homemade dog food, including its advantages, disadvantages, preparation techniques, ingredients, costs, and supplements. You will also receive practical experience and guidance. Additionally, you can network and connect with other dog owners and professionals who create homemade dog food by attending this offline session. You can also trade knowledge, guidance, and many other things.

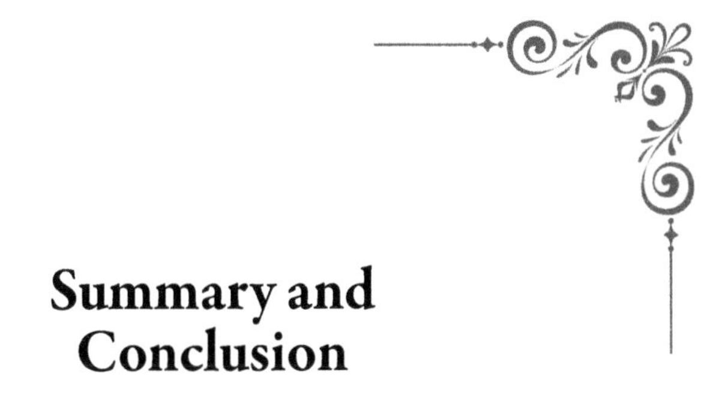

Summary and Conclusion

THIS BOOK SERVES AS a helpful manual and resource for dog owners who wish to use inexpensive, natural, and easy materials to make better, healthier, and tastier food for their pets. More than eighty-five recipes for homemade dog food that is full, balanced, and ideal for all breeds, ages, and health conditions are included in this book, along with recipes for treats, supplements, and snacks. This book offers guidance and information on the advantages, dangers, and techniques of preparing homemade dog food in addition to discussing dogs' dietary requirements and preferences and the ideal ways to prepare and store it.

The primary objective of this book is to assist dog owners in providing their pets with food that is not only tasty but also nourishing and advantageous to their overall health and well-being, so enhancing both the quality and quantity of their dogs' lives. According to the author, homemade dog food has a lot of benefits over store-bought dog food, including:

Compared to commercial dog food, homemade dog food may be fresher, more natural, and more personalized. You may customize homemade dog food to your dog's requirements and tastes by selecting the ingredients, amounts, and supplements. Additionally, homemade dog food can assist you in avoiding certain chemicals, additives, or allergies that can be found in some commercial dog food.

Purchasing dog food in bulk or during a sale, together with using seasonal, local, or organic ingredients, can result in cheaper homemade dog food than store-bought dog food. Because homemade dog food can prevent or treat some common health issues in dogs, such allergies, obesity, diabetes, or arthritis, it can also help you save money on veterinary expenditures.

For you and your dog, homemade dog food might be more enjoyable and fulfilling than store-bought dog food. By taking the time and making the food yourself, you can show your dog how much you care and how much you love him. By giving your dog homemade dog food, you may strengthen your relationship and engage with him by sharing meals and treats.

But the author also notes that making dog food at home has drawbacks and restrictions, like:

Compared to commercial dog food, homemade dog food needs more time, work, and expertise. It might take a lot of time and energy to plan, prepare, shop, make, and store homemade dog food on a regular basis. It might be challenging and perplexing to make sure homemade dog food satisfies your dog's nutritional needs and standards.

Not every dog or circumstance will benefit from homemade dog food. particular dogs might be allergic to particular components, have dietary restrictions that call for expert advice, or both. Some circumstances, like traveling, boarding, or an emergency, can prevent you from making or feeding homemade dog food.

As a result, the author suggests that dog owners seek assistance from their veterinarian and be practical and adaptable while preparing homemade dog food. In order to have the best of both worlds, the author also advises dog owners to blend homemade and commercial dog food, giving their pets a combination of the two or switching between them.

The book's author believes that dog owners will be motivated and empowered to feed their pets more healthfully and to take pleasure in the preparation and end product of homemade dog food. In addition, the author hopes that this book will promote longer, happier, and healthier lives for dog owners and their pets. As the book comes to an end, the author states:

"Better dog food doesn't have to be difficult, costly, or time-consuming to prepare. It can be inexpensive, simple, and enjoyable. All you really need is a little bit of imagination, education, and love. And the benefits are incalculable. Your dog will express his gratitude to you with his sparkling eyes, shining coat, wagging tail, and unwavering love. And you'll be glad that you fed your closest friend the greatest cuisine you could."

Don't miss out!

Visit the website below and you can sign up to receive emails whenever Daniel J. Sanford publishes a new book. There's no charge and no obligation.

https://books2read.com/r/B-A-JXOBB-WLWQC

BOOKS 2 READ

Connecting independent readers to independent writers.

Milton Keynes UK
Ingram Content Group UK Ltd.
UKHW020233301123
433483UK00016B/945